Beyond Breathing

Margarete Cassalina

Dear Tricia,

Thank You!

Breathe,
Margarete Cassalina

iUniverse Star
New York   Bloomington

Beyond Breathing

iUniverse Star
an iUniverse, Inc. imprint

iUniverse books may be ordered through booksellers or by contacting:

iUniverse
1663 Liberty Drive
Bloomington, IN 47403
www.iuniverse.com
1-800-Authors (1-800-288-4677)

ISBN: 978-1-935278-57-3 (pbk)
ISBN: 978-1-935278-65-8 (cloth)
ISBN: 978-1-935278-58-0 (ebk)

Printed in the United States of America

Library of Congress Control Number: 2009925174

iUniverse Rev. Date 3/24/2009

Dedication

To God's grace, His gift, my daughter, Jena; in so many ways
you left us breathless …

Introduction

"On Monday, December 4, 2006, at 9:57 AM, my beautiful daughter, Jena Marie Cassalina, lost her life to cystic fibrosis. She was thirteen."

The first time I wrote those words, I looked down and saw my worn blue rubber CF awareness bracelet. The inscribed word, *breathe,* stared at me, almost mocking me. Breathe, it said. Breathing was something Jena was no longer doing and breathing was something I was finding so hard to do. It was just one breath that kept me from my daughter. Jena was beyond breathing. Breathing, I now know, is something way overrated.

Chapter 1

When I was a child, my mother drilled into my psyche that education and self-interest were all that was important in life; that marriage and children were obstacles that deterred you from the sole purpose of getting ahead. She once told me that if you needed a man in your life you were worthless and weak. She explained that men were crutches and that strong women didn't require them. She made it clear that stay-at-home mothers did so because they could not "make it" and that they served no purpose in the real world. She would refer to stay-at-home mothers—and still does—as morons or bimbos.

Ironically, it was only after I became a mother that I turned into a "somebody."

My parents finally divorced when I was in eighth grade after having spent my entire life fighting, living together, moving apart, and moving back in together over and over, year after year. It was February 6, 1982, and I had been living with my grandparents—my father's parents—in Peru, New York, when I got the phone call. They were officially divorced. That was the extent of it. My father called to inform me of their decision. He didn't talk long; after all, it was a long-distance call. Mercifully, I was placed in a stable environment, with Oma and Opa, for one year. I'd like to think my parents had me live with my grandparents for *my* emotional benefit and not theirs, but I still have my doubts. My parents couldn't handle a dissolving marriage, two teenagers, and a three-year-old boy.

In fact, the year after I moved back home to New York, I was sent to Worms, Germany, to live with my great-aunt, Thea, for a "culture experience." Again, I doubt it was for my benefit but anything had to be better than being home. Regardless of the intent, I did have a "cultural experience" and, despite my preconceived opinion, I did have a wonderful time. The rumor in my high school, started by small-minded parents, was that I went to Worms to have a baby. Ha! I was a fat fourteen-year-old who had a dysfunctional family life! Instead of any understanding from small-town minds, I had more issues to deal with.

It was in Germany that I learned to smoke cigarettes and drink wine. Great *cultural* experience. My dad had already moved out of the house for the last time in 1982, leaving the house for my mother to raise Evelyn, Matthew, and me. My father moved back in with his parents in Peru, financially broke, with nothing but his clothes and his car. I believe he figured we—my brother Matt, my sister Evelyn, and I—had gone through enough and thought perhaps things would settle down if we stayed together in the house with my mother. Unfortunately, that didn't happen. At this point, however, I really think he tried to do right by us.

By the time I came back from Germany, my sister Evelyn, who was eighteen, had moved out of my mother's house and into an apartment with a guy named Angelo. Ev had enough and thought perhaps she'd be better living on her own than living with my mother. But I am just guessing here.

At age four, my little brother Matt moved to Oma and Opa's house for more of the same stability I had achieved in eighth grade. Oma and Opa would watch Matt Monday through Friday, and my dad, now living in a house of his own, would take Matt on weekends. Matt grew up basically without my mother's influence, except for those occasional bursts of guilty maternal un-instincts that would erupt every now and then.

When I was fifteen, back home in New York, I returned from my friend Debbie's house and found my mother sitting on the couch drinking shots of vodka and "toasting" the air: "Here's to the death of my daughter." It was her melodramatic way of stating that her relationship with Evelyn was over. They were no longer speaking and apparently this was her way of dealing with it.

I will always remember that because it was proof that everyone in her life was expendable; I knew I was next in line.

Even though I was on track to graduate from high school a year early, my grades weren't as great as they once had been. My mother and I argued about education, my future, and, most of all, my friends. I disappointed her by going to Dutchess Community College instead of to elite Vassar College, where she had graduated. In June 1985, I was sixteen and I had been dating a guy named Dave who was four years older than I was. My mother never called him by his name; she only referred to him as "asshole." I got the brunt of her anger, since I was the only one left in her house. Emotionally, I was on edge. Every time I walked up the front steps, I would throw up over the porch railing before I could even open the front door.

My mother and I were about to have our last argument. She was pretty certain I wouldn't be going to Vassar College any time soon and I think she was afraid I would wind up pregnant and married to "asshole." It was a hot day in June when I walked in the front door for the last time. She was in one of her moods. I don't remember what it was all about. I just remember thinking we seriously needed help. I screamed at her, "I can't take living like this anymore!"

She said, "Well, you know where the door is." She walked over, opened the door, and just stood there. Crying, I ran upstairs to my room, put all my clothes in a hefty garbage bag, and left. I never looked back. I never went in her house again.

I moved into Dave's house with him and his mother, who called my father and told him what was going on. I had my own room and I paid her $350 each month. I worked as a waitress and bartender to pay for my car, college, and room and board. Nothing was given to me, certainly not self-esteem. The only thing I knew for sure was that I wasn't worth much to anyone. My relationship with Dave only lasted a few years. He may not have been the "asshole" my mother thought, but he certainly wasn't the answer I had hoped he'd be.

By the time I met Marc, I was twenty-one, my family was scattered, and I was a mess. I had maintained a relationship with my dad, who was now happily married to Sherry, and they were raising Matthew together. My sister, Evelyn, was going back to school at Plattsburgh State after her seven-month marriage to David had ended. My mother was somewhere in Europe or the Philippines—I am not exactly sure which—and I heard she'd gotten married again. We were slowly moving forward as a family, without my mother.

My friend Debbie, whom I have known since I was three, has seen me through all the phases of my life and, regardless of all my dysfunction, is still one of my closest friends. She lived four houses down from me on Innis Avenue in Poughkeepsie. Debbie introduced me to Marc, who operated cranes for her stepfather's business at Gloede Neon Signs while going to college.

What stole my heart was talking with him long hours at a bar called *Let's Dance*. We talked about movies, life, and dreams. We had nice conversations, but we were not each other's type. I thought he was too young and too much of a ladies' man for me and he thought I was, well, a little too heavy. We never really could pinpoint what the attraction was between us, only that there was most certainly a strong one. Marc would ask out every pretty female in sight and then eventually would get to me. I'd pass on his offer. After all, I did have *some* self-respect.

Then one Tuesday evening in August, Debbie gave him my phone number and he called. After a long conversation, I agreed to go to dinner with him that Friday night. Marc picked me up and took me to dinner at Foster's Coach House Restaurant on August 11, 1989, and we have been together ever since.

Marc, at twenty-two, had just graduated from Marist College and was working at Merrill Lynch when I found out I was pregnant. The date was November 10, 1990. I was a secular German-Irish nonconformist, product of two generations of divorce. Marc was from a large, conservative, Italian Catholic family. As it would turn out, the only thing our families had in common was fatal.

When I was three months along, on January 12, 1991, we got married. We lived next door to Marc's family and had Sunday dinner with them every week. I thought this new obstacle, my pregnancy, would be the end of the "somebody" I was meant to be. I would now become the moron or the bimbo my mother had so fervently warned me about.

Chapter 2

It's positive.

My whole life I had always thought *positive* was a good word. Webster's dictionary defines it as "favorable." And when seven doctors at Westchester Medical Center walked into my newborn son's neonatal ICU room and told me that Eric had tested positive, my first reaction was, "Great! Now let me take him home."

Slow down, not so fast.

Eric was born with meconium ileus, a blockage in the intestines that usually comes out during childbirth. His didn't. I was still recovering from having him at Vassar Brothers Hospital in Poughkeepsie when I was asked by the doctor on call to pick either Albany Medical Center or Westchester Medical Center because Eric needed to be flown to one of them immediately. I looked at Marc, who looked back at me and then at the anxious, waiting physician and blurted out "Westchester."

Two people in red flight suits walked in and put Eric in a small, clear box called an isolette with wires hooked up to him. They whisked Eric off to a waiting helicopter.

I discharged myself, and Marc and I drove by car to meet Eric at Westchester Medical Center which was over an hour away. He was already in the Neonatal Intensive Care Unit (NICU) by the time we arrived. They ran tests for two days, trying to figure out what was wrong with my baby boy. Finally they had one more test to give him: a sweat test.

Marc and I were in our sterile yellow garments in the NICU. I was rocking Eric in the rocking chair, staring at him. His tiny hand grasped my pinky. He was swaddled in the hospital blanket, which did a poor job of hiding all the wires that were attached to him.

Dr. Doom, the only woman of the seven doctors who had trooped in, reached for my hand when she said that Eric had tested positive. Still, it didn't compute. "The tests are positive. Your child has cystic fibrosis."

Marc looked at me and then at the solemn faces of the rest of the doctors. That is when I realized that *positive* is not always a good thing. Eric had tested positive for cystic fibrosis, and that was not a good thing.

Cystic fibrosis (CF) was unknown to me—a new mom who had just given birth three days ago. What was CF? How did Eric get CF? How can we get rid of CF? Is CF bad? One sentence from Dr. Doom would sum it all up for me.

"CF is a fatal genetic disease."

I certainly understood those words. For the next three hours, the seven doctors went on to explain everything we never wanted to know about CF. They told us that cystic fibrosis is a genetic disease that affects the lungs and digestive tract. They told us that CF causes the body to produce thick mucus that clogs the airways, enabling bacteria to grow, which often leads to life-threatening lung damage. What a nice way to say *death*. They told us that the mucus exists throughout the body, causing the pancreas, reproductive organs, and sometimes the liver not to function to full capacity. They tried to ease our fear by telling us that the pancreatic issue can be controlled with oral enzyme supplements, but added that, unfortunately, 70 percent of all people with cystic fibrosis eventually get cystic fibrosis–related diabetes (CFRD).

For the most up-to-date information on cystic fibrosis, go to the Therapeutic Drug Pipeline at the www.cff.org web site.

Breathe, I told myself. *Breathe.*

The doctors started getting more detailed and explained that Marc and I were unknowing genetic carriers of the CF gene found in chromosome seven. We'd had a 25 percent chance of having a child with CF. Back in 1989, scientists had isolated the cystic fibrosis gene, and they are working on gene therapy and, ultimately, the cure for the disease.

They had my full, undivided attention when they disclosed to us that Eric's life expectancy was nineteen. I was twenty-two. Marc and I had fallen in love with Eric the moment he was born. It was then that I knew my mother knew nothing about being one.

When my father, his wife Sherry, and my sister Evelyn heard about the diagnosis, they made the five-hour drive from Plattsburgh to be there with us and my in-laws in the neonatal intensive care unit at Westchester Medical Center. They were in as much shock as we were about what CF meant. Not surprisingly, there was no comment, call, or visit from my mother. I don't even know if she knew I was married.

Chapter 3

Ironically, when I thought I was giving up "me," I gradually started to know that I was truly alive and recognized who I was. I had thought my life and all my dreams were over. I thought all I had planned for would end.

Being pregnant with Eric taught me the first of many life lessons I would learn from my kids that I would never be able to repay. It took me Eric's whole pregnancy to contemplate the wonder of creating a life. In time, I began to understand the priceless value of a mother and a wife; for me that was a new concept.

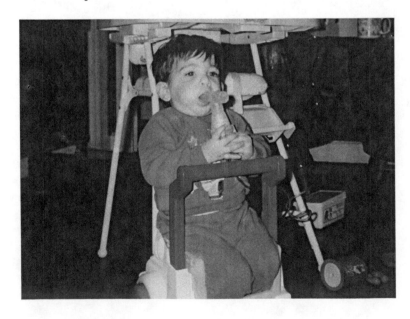

Raising Eric and learning about cystic fibrosis consumed all my time. I created a basic schedule for his eating, sleeping, and playing. I had to schedule in his breathing treatments three times a day, physical therapy three times a day, medicine hidden in his baby food at every meal, and endless doctor's appointments an hour away. And I made absolutely sure we scheduled in fun things to do—just the two of us—while Marc worked twelve-hour days and seventy-hour weeks.

Still, Marc and I meshed perfectly. We only had one car and one paycheck and we considered ourselves successful. During Marc's first weeks at Merrill Lynch, the office manager had asked the rookies if any of them considered themselves successful. Marc was the only one who raised his hand. Marc was also the only one in the room who didn't consider money the only way of measuring success.

Eric was a great baby. I would put him in the stroller and walk into town just to get out of the house. When he got older, we would walk alongside the tiny brook that flowed down the road where we lived. Eric would throw a stick or a twig in the brook and chase it as fast as his little legs would go. He and I were alone most of the time. My friends were still in college and caught up in the full swing of college life and being single. Eric and I did not get many visits and, without a car, we didn't go many places, either.

I looked forward to Sundays, since it was the only day I was sure I would have company and a good meal. We spent every Sunday at my in-laws for their traditional Italian Sunday macaroni dinner. We still do that today.

By the time Eric was eleven months old, he was doing very well by medical standards. No problems. No lung damage. No complications. We thought perhaps CF wasn't as bad as everyone was making it out to be. Perhaps we would be different. We were young and ambitious. We were in love and a team. We thought we had the right attitude and fortitude. We thought we could conquer it all. We also thought it was easy to breathe.

Statistically speaking, we had a 25 percent chance of having a child with CF, a 50 percent chance the child would just be a carrier like Marc and me, and a 25 percent chance the child wouldn't have even the gene. Perhaps we would defy the odds. Perhaps it was easy to breathe. I am not sure if we were naive about CF, or if it was just that we had trust in God.

We knew we wanted another child and just prayed God knew what He was doing. Marc and I each took a deep breath, looked at each other, and Marc said, "I hope it's a girl."

Chapter 4

It was hailed as the "Storm of the Century" by weathermen around the country. Here in our little town of Milton, New York, on March 13, 1993, we were in a state of emergency due to high winds and whiteout conditions. Only four-wheel drive emergency vehicles were allowed on the roads, and the bridge was closed. There were twenty-eight inches of snow already on the ground, with six-foot snowdrifts, and it was still coming down heavily. I was nine months pregnant and safe at my in-laws' house until my water broke. *Insert curse word here.*

Eric, now nineteen months old, had been born only thirteen minutes after my water broke. The hospital was fifteen minutes away on a good day, and I had to cross the Mid-Hudson Bridge, which was now closed because of the blizzard.

Inhale ... two... three ... four ...
Exhale ... two ... three ... four ...

Remarkably, we made it to Vassar Brothers Hospital in record time in Marc's old, beat-up three-quarter-ton rusted pickup truck. Fortunately, it had a snowplow. Marc had to plow our way to the bridge, where we explained to the nice bridge authority man that we just *had* to get to the hospital. He and Marc bantered back and forth a few moments until the guy got one look at me and let us go without another word. We plowed the bridge and made it to the hospital in thirty-two minutes, where we had our own "Storm of the Century."

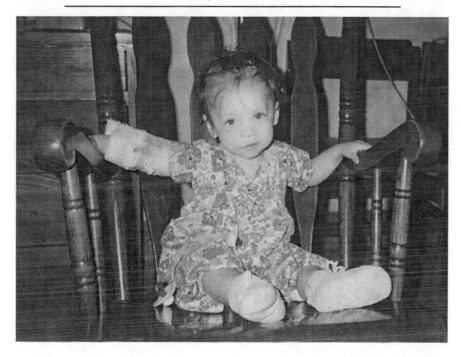

Jena Marie Cassalina was born Saturday night at 11:02 PM. One boy, one girl; our family was complete.

It was positive. This time I knew it wasn't good. Jena's second sweat test also came back positive. Jena, at one month, was diagnosed with cystic fibrosis, that fatal genetic disease. We had two kids, both with CF, and still there was no cure.

Chapter 5

Breathe

I remembered a poem I had read once about how children learn what they live. I wanted my children to live life to the fullest, so that is what I intended to teach them. They had CF, but that was never going to define who they were. Not our kids. After all, I was going to teach them so much about what life is about. I was determined to have their childhoods be better than mine, CF or not.

I had a daily schedule divided into fifteen-minute increments starting at five thirty in the morning and ending at ten at night. I wanted to fit a full life into very hectic days. Having two kids with cystic fibrosis was more demanding than anyone might realize. And to fit some *me* time into the day was almost impossible; hence the fifteen-minute planner. Eric, nineteen months older than Jena, had a moderate expression of cystic fibrosis, as the doctors like to classify it, while Jena's expression was more severe.

I loved being home with them. I knew how important our time together was. "Budman" and "Sweet Stuff" were all I could have ever wished for. I took being a parent very seriously and educated myself along the way with as many books on parenting as I could possibly read. There were so many things to know and do in life; there were so many things I could explain to them—me, the ever-informed parent. In time, it became clear that I was the one who was taught the most. It would be me who needed to learn to live life to the fullest. It would be me who would have so many new lessons to learn, and who would be taught by my kids. I had no idea how painfully sweet that would be.

Eric was born to be a fantastic big brother. He would help me however he could. He would shake the rattle in front of Jena to keep her quiet while I got their medicine and food together. He would give her back her blanket if he noticed that Jena had tossed it to the ground, and he would push her binky back into her mouth any time she started to get fussy.

Jena adored her big brother from the beginning. All Eric had to do was walk by and Jena's arms and legs would flail with glee. At six months, Jena would smile and squeal every time she saw her brother come near her. He'd look at her sitting in her swing and give her a quick push and go on playing trucks. He gave her just enough time to keep her happy without taking too much time away from doing what he wanted to do.

Doing chest physical therapy took thirty minutes twice a day for each kid; organizing their medicine, their food intake, exercise, and naps took all my time. Yet we still made time for walks into town. Marc was doing better financially at Merrill Lynch, and we had just purchased land next to my in-laws to build our dream home. Everything seemed to be moving in the right direction.

Chapter 6

Breathe

We did spend time with friends. I had my girlfriends—Cindy, Jo-Ann, Joanne, and Tara—and Marc spent time with his friends (Mike, John D., and Marc's cousin John B.). All our friends got along. We traveled with the kids every vacation we could and moved forward in designing a life we wanted, rather than accepting the one that had been handed to us.

When there was a day off from school, the question asked was never "What are we doing?" but rather "Where are we going?" It was a standing rule in our house that any and all days off from school meant going someplace—any place. Marc and I have always loved to travel, and Jena had apparently inherited that travel gene.

Eric loved to play games and be with the family but never quite cared where that would take place. Jena didn't care where it was either, but she had a great desire to do it somewhere other than Milton. Therefore, we did. It was easy when the kids were young, but once CF took its toll on them, it got harder to go places. We had a bunch of plastic gadgets and tubing, along with machines for both kids to help them do their breathing treatments. Jena had bags, formulas, and machines for her feeding tube, which was hooked up at night, and eventually an oxygen concentrator to help her breathe. Both kids had diabetes, and we now needed to refrigerate medicine, along with hard plastic containers to keep needles safe and stored. We had more medicine and medical equipment than would fit in a suitcase. Still, our famous promise to the kids was, "We'll make it happen."

No one was surprised when Marc bought a thirty-five-foot motor home that bore the appropriate logo, "Roughing it smoothly," and roughing it smoothly we did. We replaced air travel with road travel. We traveled to thirty-five states across America, never letting CF slow us down. We took friends on vacation with us, we took family, and we even took the kids' IV antibiotics with us on a few trips in lieu of a stay at Club Med. I had gotten so knowledgeable in the way of running an IV and doing the kids' meds that I felt I had gotten my medical degree through on-the-job training. I never went to medical school, but I did spend more time in a hospital than any intern I knew. Not the road I was planning on going down, but I was never going to let CF stand in the way of living. The kids made sure of that.

With the RV, we camped at great places with swimming pools, campfires, and minigolf. Eric's rule of thumb was that it was never a vacation unless we lit something on fire, and Jena's was that we had to play minigolf. We camped in state parks and people's driveways, but the place we stayed the most was in an RV/truck stop all across America called the "Flying J." We stayed at Flying J's because we were always on our way somewhere from someplace and just needed to crash. It is a great place to chat with other RVers—who I think are just the friendliest people—and refuel, recharge, and dump you-know-what. We have stayed at every Flying J east of the Mississippi.

Chapter 7

When Jena was three, I asked her what she wanted to wear for preschool. Her choice was purple and pink–striped socks, a large, brightly multicolored flowered skirt, and a too-small canary yellow tank top with a fuchsia hand-knitted heart pattern sweater to top it all off. Mortified at her combination, not realizing the problem was really my insecurities as a mother, I told her she couldn't wear such a ridiculous outfit out in public. I mean really, what *would* everyone think? Jena never cared about such a simpleminded approach. Jena knew who she was. It was I who didn't have a clue. I tried logic on her to dissuade her from her drastic choice of clothing. Have you ever tried to argue logically with a three-year-old? Needless to say, there were tears and screaming, and the outcome was that we both gave in and neither of us was happy.

Jena had taught me compromise. I also picked up a few parenting skills that helped me in the future. One was to give her a choice between two outfits that I had picked and to make sure I considered Jena's taste when choosing them, rather than mine. We never fought about clothes again.

Breathe

Kids can accumulate a lot of toys—or *junk,* as Marc and I like to say—and in five years, our house was no exception. The kids' toys spilled over from the living room into the hallway and all over the kitchen. As parents trying to teach the kids responsibility for taking care of their own junk—I mean toys—we expected Eric and Jena to pick up their toys when they were through playing with them. Apparently, Jena must have missed that family memo because she had no intention of cleaning up. We even sang the "clean up" song to encourage the "fun" of being responsible. still, to no avail, Jena refused. So, as any parent would do, we showed her how to pick up, whether she wanted to or not. I took her little hands and walked with her to the small wooden chair she had left in the other room. I sternly helped her carry the chair back to its rightful place. Jena followed along for a moment, looked at me, then the chair, and finally pulled her hands out from underneath mine and grabbed the seat of the chair. With all her three-year-old might, she threw it forcefully back where she had been using it, where it landed on its side. At that moment, I knew for sure that my little girl had unshakable determination.

Although her approach was wrong, what I did learn from Jena was that she was not through with her chair just quite yet. Ignoring me, she walked over to the sideways chair and placed it upright. With her back toward me, she sat in her chair for a few minutes, stared intently at the bare wall and then at her feet, which were swinging carelessly under her. I could see her trying to look at me from the corner of her eyes. She sat there another minute and then got up and returned the chair to its proper place when *she* was ready.

What I learned that day was that I should understand her needs before I made her understand mine. I realized then that perhaps the world does not function in "my time" and that the same result can still be obtained if I take a moment to understand others' needs. I have to admit that did not solve our problems of cleaning up; we still had issues in that area—oh boy, did we ever!

Me too.

It was Eric and "me too." Like it or not, Jena would have to do everything Eric did. She idolized his every move. As she grew, she would have to play with everything he did. When he got a bike, she had to have one; when he got to go somewhere, so did she. Eric wasn't a big fan of the little sister "me-too" business, but he took it in stride.

Chapter 8

My whole life I have been on a diet. I can't recall a day when I didn't think about calories, fat, or cellulite. When I was growing up, the childhood nickname my petite, thin mom gave me was "Butterball." My dad's term of endearment for me was "Pork Chop." My sister Evelyn once asked me why I even bothered to eat the ice cream I was holding: why not just rub it on my thighs, since it was going there anyway? I was seven inches taller, three years younger, and many pounds heavier than Evelyn was, and she would never, ever let me forget it.

The most hurtful nickname was "TNT," which I was dubbed in high school by a bunch of popular boys who reminded me that it wasn't because I was *dynamite;* it was "T and T" because I had Thunder Thighs. The boys would walk behind me making the sound of the earth shaking with every step I took.

This was what I brought to the table as a parent. I had no idea how to deal with the fact that my daughter was *not* gaining weight at all and that the lack of weight gain was now life-threatening.

Jena was five years old and weighed twenty-eight pounds when she should have weighed forty. She had weighed that for the past eighteen months, and the doctors were not happy. Marc and I had been diligently trying to hide calories in her food. I made things with heavy cream and butter, I only bought Häagen-Dazs ice cream, and I used weight-gain powder in her milk. I gained at least fifteen pounds, but Jena did not gain a single ounce.

Dr. Boyer told us we couldn't wait any more; her health and growth were being severely compromised. He wanted to surgically put a gastrostomy tube—a G-tube—in her stomach so we could "feed" her while she slept. Dr.

B. told us that there really wasn't any other choice. More facts about cystic fibrosis that I never wanted to know.

On Eric's seventh birthday—July 17, 1998—Jena went in for her second surgery. The first surgery had been to reconstruct her submucus cleft; this one was for her G-tube. It was not a good day. Eric spent his birthday with Ann, my mother-in-law, while Marc and I spent the day with Jena at Westchester Medical Center in Valhalla, New York. Over the years, we spent so much time there that we ironically called it "Club Med" and were on a first-name basis with almost everyone who dealt with pediatrics.

That particular morning at Westchester began with tears as the nurses tried to get an IV into Jena's arm. She fought needles as fiercely as she fought to live. She would scream until she broke blood vessels all over the surface of her skin, but she would never move. Never. She knew moving would mean another stick, and that just would not happen. By 11 AM they told us it was time for her surgery, and I needed to sign a bunch of papers before they would bring her downstairs to the Operating Room (OR).

After I put on "visitor scrubs," I was able to go into the OR with Jena. I was able to hold her hand until she either cried herself to sleep or the sedation in her IV made her unconscious. Either way it was heartbreaking. I kissed her on the cheek, told her I loved her, and then the OR nurse escorted me out into the hallway where Marc was already pacing. As I took off my pseudodoctor garments and put them in the designated bin, I looked back through the small glass window where Jena appeared to be asleep. It took two nurses, two anesthesiologists, and two surgeons to do this "minor" procedure, as they had previously told me. *They* never understood that nothing about Jena was ever "minor."

Marc and I sat on the newly buffed cement floor outside the operating room for four hours before the pediatric surgeon came out into the hallway to tell us that he was done embedding the feeding tube in her stomach. Dr. Stringel was the chief pediatric surgeon at Westchester Medical Center.

Dr. Stringel further explained that they had found it necessary to do a bronchoscopy to expel the mucus from Jena's lungs while she was under anesthesia. He told us that Jena's lungs were full of phlegm and this had been a good opportunity to "clean" them out. They had scraped, sucked, and rinsed her lungs from the inside. We didn't know that would be the first of six bronchoscopies she would endure. Dr. Stringel told us that Jena was just waking up in the recovery room and we could go in, but he warned us that she was in a lot of pain.

I will never forget the look on her face when she saw me. At first it was relief that I was there and the next it was sheer pain and confusion. She tried to cough, but when she did she grabbed her throat with her hands, and her blue eyes winced in pain. She sounded hoarse and sore when she cried, *"Mommy!"* She had no idea what was going on and she was forced to recover from everything I had signed off on that morning. How could I explain to her that this was to help her? That I did this because I love her, and that this was going to make things better for her? All I could do was hold her tiny little hand and tell her I loved her and that it was all going to be OK. I never intentionally lied to her; I didn't even know I was lying to myself.

Mercifully, the OR nurse gave her more sedation in her IV, and she dozed off for a while. It was enough time for me to get my thoughts together. While she was sleeping, I saw what I had done. There was a six-inch rubber tube protruding from a large patch of sterile gauze that was taped tightly to her belly. The gauze was deceptively clean. It looked like everything was fine except for the tears pouring down my face, which told me differently. *What had I done?* The other end of the six-inch rubber tube was attached to a clear bag that was hung at the edge of her bed. It was filling up with watery blood and some green phlegm. The nurse explained that it was drainage from her stomach and that would continue for a few hours. I looked at her belly and saw dark red blood slowly devouring the once-white sterile gauze. I thought I was going to be sick.

The hospital had stopped serving dinner by the time Marc and I got Jena to her room on the third floor. I was grateful that the nurse down in the recovery room had changed the blood-soaked gauze they call "dressing" while Jena was still groggy. She was fully awake by now. Pam, her pediatric nurse, found some cherry Italian ice for her to suck on and Jena was once again—remarkably—smiling. She always amazed me.

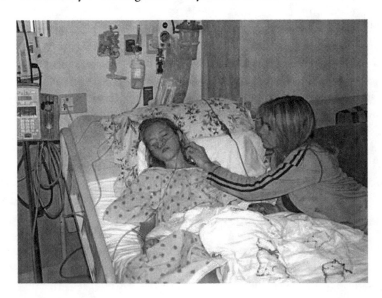

Marc was making jokes about how, if she held her nose and mouth shut, she could fill up a balloon through her stomach, and Jena wanted to call Eric to wish him a happy birthday.

We brought Jena home on July 22. The name of the plastic device left surgically implanted in her stomach was a MIC-KEY button. Each night Jena would put three cans of Nutren 2.0 formula—a total of twenty-four ounces and 1,500 calories—into a plastic bag that had a few feet of rubber tubing and attach that to her Mickey button. It would be regulated by a Kangaroo Pump machine, so she would receive the calories throughout the night while she slept. The smell of the formula was putrid, and many nights she would vomit curdles of it. We would have to change all the sheets, do laundry in the middle of the night, and start the machine again. Eventually, she was diagnosed with GERD (gastroesophageal reflux disease). Still, Jena did it every night because she knew she had to.

By the beginning of August, she had gained five pounds, celebrated by the tiny roll that formed when she stuck her stomach out as she bent forward. Stomach rolls in our family were grounds for celebration.

Jena never did quite get above the tenth percentile in weight, but she knew the feeding tube was necessary, even though she couldn't blow up a balloon through the hole in her stomach.

Chapter 9

Somewhere along the way, I became a dedicated volunteer for the Cystic Fibrosis Foundation. Two marvelous women were instrumental in the success of creating the Cystic Fibrosis Foundation. After being told there was no foundation for cystic fibrosis and no help and no research to be found to save her little girl's life, Doris Tulcin helped to create the Cystic Fibrosis Foundation, along with other CF parents. Mary Weiss constructed a model for CF awareness and worked with Doris to raise millions of dollars to fund research.

Doris has been fighting CF since 1957, shortly after her infant daughter Annie was diagnosed with the disease.

They were visionaries, they were a force, and they were both moms to kids with CF. They became my rock stars, my "Bono," my American Idol.

Mary Weiss is best known for her "sixty-five roses" story. Mary became a volunteer for the Cystic Fibrosis Foundation in 1965 after learning that her three little boys had CF. Her duty was to call every civic club and social and service organization seeking financial support for CF research. Mary's four-year-old son, Richard, listened closely to his mother as she made each call.

After several calls, Richard came into the room and told his mom, "I know what you are working for." Mary was dumbstruck because Richard did not know what she was doing, nor did he know that he had cystic fibrosis. With some trepidation, Mary asked, "What am I working for, Richard?" He answered, "You are working for sixty-five roses." Mary was speechless.

He could not see the tears running down Mary's cheeks as she stammered, "Yes Richard, I'm working for sixty-five roses."

Since 1965, the term "sixty-five roses" has been used by children of all ages to describe their disease. The "sixty-five roses" story has captured the hearts and emotions of all who have heard it. The rose, appropriately the ancient symbol of love, has become a symbol of the Cystic Fibrosis Foundation (from the CFF Web site).

At a CF conference in Texas, back in 2000, I was explaining to a few other volunteers how I am always creating opportunities to share my story of CF and create more awareness. I told them how I always wear a CF shirt to the gym, that I have a one-of-a-kind tattoo of a rose with "CF" in the thorns, and I have a license plate that says "65 Roses," which lends itself to interesting conversations with people.

After I was done, a woman came up to me and asked about my license plate. I began to explain about the "sixty-five roses" story and she ever so politely smiled at me and didn't interrupt a word I said. When I was done, I put out my hand and said, "Hi, I am Margarete Cassalina."

She smiled, looked me in the eye, shook my hand, and said, "Hi, I'm Mary Weiss."

I just about died.

"Oh my God!" I screamed. "You're Mary Weiss!"

Like she hadn't just told me that. I hugged her tightly and said again, "Oh my God! You're Mary Weiss!"

We chatted quite awhile on that trip and she has since become a dear friend to me. I am still in complete awe of all she has done, and I just love her.

One of the best compliments I ever got in my entire life was at a CF conference in Washington DC. Doris and I had a lot of energetic conversations and at one point she grabbed my hand and said, "You remind me so much of me."

Wow.

Doris does not say anything she doesn't want to, and I know that was one of the best compliments I have ever received.

Chapter 10

My mother came to visit. This was a first. It was summer and she had just moved to Prague from the Philippines and had time to accommodate her guilt trip to America. She wanted to see her three biological children. I was here in Milton, and Ev and my brother Matt lived four hours north on the thruway in Plattsburgh, New York.

If you ever had the excruciating desire to ask my mother why she is removed from her entire family, she'd tell you she just couldn't stay in this country, that she isn't from this country, and that she had no choice but to move herself halfway around the world to teach high school English. She would let you know that she and Europe were far better than anything America could produce. It is there that she felt she belonged.

She taught high school in Bangkok after she left Matt to be raised by my father. That was two years after she threw me out of the house at age sixteen, which was two years after my sister left. That was two years after she finally divorced my father, whom she has said she never wanted to marry in the first place. Which was two years after she thought having a child would save her marriage. I'd like to blame her for my genetic defect, but she has never been around to be tested.

When my mother came to visit, she had just divorced her second husband, Joe something or other, who, ironically, she said was mentally unbalanced. She was now ex Mrs. Renate Grosinski-McCord-whatever. She was in America for only one week and she made it clear how valuable her time was and how important she was to the high school she taught at somewhere in Europe. The only thing missing was the back of her hand against her forehead when she spoke.

Ignoring Eric and Jena when she talked, my mother implied to Marc that she was the most intelligent person at work and that she worked with idiots and men who just wanted her. She spoke mainly to Marc because, after all, I was a stay-at-home mother, a bimbo—of no use to the conversation.

She never knew that Marc was just dealing with her because she was my mother and because I was still yearning for some sort of relationship with her. She didn't know how his stomach turned when he looked at her because of all she has done to me.

She stayed only a few days and then went up to visit Evelyn and Matthew. Evelyn and my mother seemed to be getting along better. Evelyn had received her master's in education and was now teaching English at Plattsburgh State. I guess they now had things in common. I was still married to the same husband and squeezing in a class here and there at SUNY–New Paltz, trying to be a somebody.

The second time my mother visited, she arrived accessorized by one of her boyfriends. I can't remember his name, only that he didn't say much. Jena, eight at the time, had been practicing German for weeks, hoping to impress the never-present grandmother. When my mother arrived, I had already been drinking. She talked for hours on end and gave an occasional nod if you ever said something she considered worth listening to. It was now time for bed, and Jena had patiently waited all night to show off her German.

Standing at the far end of the dinner table, Jena announced, "Guten Nacht."

Simply translated, it means "good night" and, to this day, I wish it had been. Marc and I stopped and smiled and anxiously awaited a response from my mother, who was looking down into her almost-empty wine glass. Marc interrupted her boredom and said to Jena, "I don't think she heard you. Why don't you say it again, honey?"

Never looking up from her wine glass, uninterested in Jena's distraction, my mother coldly said, "No, I heard her," and sipped the last drop of wine.

Jena looked at the ground, defeated. I was furious. I walked with Jena upstairs, and while I set up her feeding tube, I told her she had said it perfectly. She looked so crushed. My rage had changed into compassion for Jena. I sat on her bed, holding her hands, and tried to explain that if she looked in the dictionary under "self-centered" she'd see my mother's picture, and that my mother didn't know how to interact with an adorable little girl. I apologized that "Mommy's mom" was a miserable excuse for a grandmother. Jena smiled and said that was OK because she already had a really good grandma who lived next door, and that my mother would have just been an extra one she didn't really need anyway.

I gave her a kiss and said, "Ich liebe dich."

She responded, "I love you, too. Guten Nacht."

I smiled, started her feeding tube, and walked downstairs. I filled my glass with as much wine as could possibly fit, kissed Marc good night, and went upstairs. I was done. I was done trying to explain my mother's actions and behavior to people. I was done making excuses for eccentric vocabulary and immature conduct. I was done pretending I had a mother.

The next day I dropped "Mommy's Mom" off at the nearest rental car place, where I left her to go off and wreak havoc in Plattsburgh. I called Evelyn and told her that Hurricane Renate's ETA was one o'clock. She was forewarned.

Chapter 11

Breathe

"You know, Mom, when I grow up I want to be a country singer or maybe an art teacher. Maybe I'll just do both," Jena announced when she was ten.

Jena loved to draw and make crafts. She loved to paint and loved to create. She came up with her own signature design, which was the letter J, intertwined with the letter C. "JC" was the name of the famous art-wear that she would design. She made drawings of the clothes she created, and all of them had the signature stamp of JC. "A JC original," she would call them. She would paint on plain white T-shirts and they would instantly become JC masterpieces.

Jena had style and flair. She would put together the most colorful creations, wrap a bright belt around her waist or a scarf on her head or neck and proudly wear her latest fashion. She was cool and she worked it well. I would never have the nerve to be as confident as Jena, but I was learning.

Jena also loved to sing and wanted to take singing lessons, so I called around and made it happen.

Jena's desire to sing far outweighed her ability. She would sing all the time, with or without music, with or without being on key. Her lungs could not keep up with her desire to sing, but that would never deter her from belting out every song on the radio as loud as she could possibly muster. Her voice teacher worked with her weekly and helped her control her diaphragm. Jena took every lesson seriously and tried hard to control her lungs to help her sing. Many times they would have to take a break to let CF make its rude interruption of coughing. When CF had its turn,

Jena would chime right back in, barely missing a beat. What did Eric think about the singing? He would just roll his eyes and let her belt out the songs.

Taking notice of how Jena did things makes it so hard for me to create excuses when I don't feel like following through. When I complain that I have a headache and can't work out, I think of Jena, who never would let something as trivial as that stand in her way.

Eric had longed for a four-wheeler but he had to wait until he was thirteen and had saved the money and proved himself responsible. We kept our word and at age thirteen he got a yellow Honda 300 EX four-wheeler.

At age eleven, "Me-too" decided she was ready as well. Marc and I held off for a year but finally decided Me-too could have one as well. This did not go over well with Eric at all.

Eventually, in Eric-like fashion, however, he would let her ride with him and his friends and Dane.

He would ride slower so she could go with them, he would start her four-wheeler when she couldn't, and he would make sure he rode behind her to keep her safe. He had so much patience when it came to Jena. He was the best big brother in the world. Jena would tell me this, so this I know for sure.

Eric did not have to go through surgeries as Jena did. His routine was more preventative, with quite a few medicines. He had airway clearance devices to remove the mucus in his lungs; he used bronchodilators and mucus thinning medicines, along with antibiotics to help keep the pseudomonas bacteria at bay. He would take his additional fat-soluble vitamins—A, D, E, and K—which are hard for those with CF to absorb. Eric also had to eat large numbers of calories—like 4,000 a day—just to stay on the chart at the fifteenth percentile.

Eric loved baseball. He always said he wanted to be a major league pitcher, but for the Mets, never the Yankees. Eric had the energy and the ability to do what he wanted. His lung function was far better than Jena's. He could swim under water two full lengths of our pool without coming up for air. He rarely missed school at this age because of having cystic fibrosis, while Jena missed a lot of school. But we also took them out of school to travel and see places they wanted to. Marc and I gave our kids cultural experiences too, but we shared them so we could see the joy on their faces.

I once read a poster at my local gym that has stuck with me. It stated, "Ships are safe in the harbor, but that is not what ships were made for." Every time I walked by that poster I thought of Jena. Jena was never made for restrictions. She would defy them all. Jena was full of life, full of strength, funny, and outgoing. We called her our Energizer Bunny because she just kept going and going. She was not made for IVs, hospitals, or wheelchairs. She was certainly not made to be constantly attached to an oxygen concentrator. Her body always seemed to adapt to what Jena needed it to do.

She would go to school and walk the halls without oxygen, she would walk down to the mailbox without it, and she would most certainly ride her four-wheeler without it. She kept up with her friends, Meaghan, Caitlyn, and Yoo-Nah, from Bishop Dunn School. She did this all against doctors' orders and any medical standard. She defied the predictions of what a person could do having only 19 percent lung function. She was made for adventure and not much would slow her down. She was made to live, laugh, and love. She did those things better than anyone I have ever known.

Chapter 12

"Can Jena fly?"

"Not without oxygen, she can't," I replied to Anthony.

Anthony is a friend who also belongs to an organization called the Knights of Columbus, which was in search of a family to send to Lourdes, Frances, in hope of a miracle. Anthony was hoping he could facilitate us in the miracle of finding the cure for cystic fibrosis for Eric and Jena. He wanted us to be that family. We did, too.

"So is that a 'yes'?" he asked

"We'll make it happen, Anthony. We'll make it happen," I answered.

Jeanie, the delightful woman at the Air France medical desk became a close personal friend of mine. I spoke with her almost every day for a month straight, trying to get all our medical needs accommodated. She had been there ten years and had never had a case like ours. It seems we had exceeded our medical allowance for the flight and using our portable oxygen concentrator in-flight was becoming an issue. We had needles for the diabetes, we had vials of medicine to be nebulized, and two of our machines had a battery type that was not allowed in the cabin. We would have to check it with the luggage, but we needed to neb the kids while in flight, and that was against regulations as well. We had the determination to make it happen, however, and we did.

We managed to get what we needed on our Air France flight, and the rest we packed very carefully in suitcases. We had two suitcases dedicated to medical needs, and I crossed my fingers that the forty-eight cans of formula for Jena's feeding tube would make the flight. The clothes for four people for ten days had to fit in one suitcase.

Jena was twelve years old and couldn't have been more thrilled to be flying across the Atlantic and going to France. She didn't mind that she had to wear oxygen in the airport or on the plane and that she had to be in a wheelchair the entire time. This wasn't even an open question because there was no way she had the strength to walk. Her breathing had become labored, and she was having serious trouble doing things she could do just a month before.

Two weeks earlier I had had serious doubts that we would even be able to make this trip. Her weight had gone down, her oxygen requirement had gone up, and her lungs now had a fungus growing in them, on top of the other bacteria that we just couldn't get rid of. It was September; school had just started, and here we were, taking the kids out for ten days on a trip to Europe. Coincidently, I had to have a root canal done only two days before we were scheduled to leave. How badly did we want it? One look at Jena, and we made it happen.

Breathe

The day before we left for France, Jena begged me to take her to Target to get her school supplies. She loved school and loved getting all the necessary notebooks, pens, paper, and accessories one needs to be cool in middle school. She was in seventh grade, she was determined, and she was armed with her must-have list.

On our way to Target, we chatted in the car about what we were going to do once we got to France. Jena wore her oxygen until we pulled into the parking lot. Then she turned off the tank and left it in the car. While she did that, I ran out and grabbed a shopping cart to push her in; she could not have walked to the front door, let alone through the store. The stares and comments we got from strangers had become amusing.

"Don't you think she's too big for that?" we were asked.

"Nope," I answered, and we went about our business.

Or sometimes people wouldn't be too nice about it, and they would say to Jena,

"Are you really that lazy?"

"Yup," she would answer with a shrewd smile.

Jena and I were used to looks and comments. We were also used to dealing with her coughing episodes, which would make her face turn a deep shade of red. The episodes would begin with coughing, and eventually, through tremendous effort, she would bring mucus up out of her lungs and spit it into a Dixie cup, which I always had on hand. Then she would wipe her mouth and hands with a Handi Wipe and off we went.

This is what CF is, and we were never going to allow CF to keep us home. Jena and I would just smile and ignore the ill-mannered comments. We hoped that these people would at some point in their lives look beyond what they see and question why they themselves are so angry at life.

That day at Target we bought way more supplies then Jena could possibly have used for the entire year. When we were done there, we went to a department store where I sat Jena on the dressing room bench and ran around the store finding outfit after outfit for her, including matching shoes and sneakers. She loved every minute of it, even though I could see that trying on clothes was wearing her out. We quickly finished our selections and I gave Jena a piggyback ride with both arms loaded down with shoes and clothes and a must-have laptop bag. As I was walking toward the register, a little boy looked up at us and said, "Boy, lady, are you strong!" Jena and I just giggled.

I spent a bundle that day, but it was my way of trying to feel better about what Jena was going through. I knew money and things couldn't relieve my pain, but if I could make her happy or smile a little brighter, it eased my heart, and I would have gladly paid with my life if I could have. That day when we got back in the car, Jena was gasping for breath. I turned the oxygen tank on a liter higher and hastily gave her the nasal canula so she could breathe easier. I watched her press her lips tightly together while she took a deep breath in through her nose. I saw her throat cave in for air while her chest expanded to get the most oxygen. I could see the pulse in her neck racing. Jena did this for a few minutes while I just looked at her in wonder.

When she seemed to be breathing easier, I asked her, my voice trembling as I spoke, "How do you do it?" My eyes welled up with tears. "You should have just stayed home. I could have gotten all this for you."

She looked at me; her lips weren't as blue as they had been two minutes before, and her breathing wasn't as labored. She gave me a fierce stare, as though she was pretending to be angry, and, with her hands on her hips, she said, "No way! I had a great time!"

I started crying. I didn't mean to, but I just couldn't understand how she could think this was fun. I kept thinking, *How much longer can she go on like this? How long do I have with her?* My worst thought yet: *how will I ever live without her?*

I stared at her in disbelief and asked her again, knowing I was selfishly asking for myself, "Jen, *how* do you do it?"

She knew what I was thinking; she knew my heart. She knew how to take care of me. I felt so guilty that I couldn't hold it together. I wanted to be strong like that little boy had said I was, but I just couldn't any more.

Jena looked at me and simply said, "I don't worry about tomorrow today. I am not going to ruin today because tomorrow I might be sad. If I am sad tomorrow, I'll be sad then, but I won't take away the fun of today."

That was my Jena. That's why she was so amazing. That changed me in an instant. That is when I was sure I would live without regret and live in the here and now, because that is where she lived. She was the best teacher I ever had.

Chapter 13

Somehow we managed to leave for France the next day. Jena, Marc, Eric, and I—and all our luggage—arrived at the airport on time and left for France. Alan and Ann, Marc's parents, joined us.

We had planned detours off the main itinerary, at our own expense, to accommodate the sites and experiences we wanted to have. Once in Paris, Jena just had to see the Mona Lisa, I just had to have a crêpe at an outside café, and Alan just had to see Notre Dame. We made it through Charles de Gaulle Airport security with only minor setbacks. We loaded down the rented van with oxygen tanks, medical equipment, and Jena's wheelchair, ready to take on France.

We went to the Eiffel Tower; we leisurely strolled down the Champs Elysée, and we got to stare directly into the eyes of the Mona Lisa in the Louvre. It was incredible and we took hundreds of pictures of fabulous memories to prove it.

After driving eight hours south of Paris, we made it to Lourdes. Here we met up with the rest of the tour. We were now on a tight schedule and the tour was, mercifully, in English. We had Mass every day, and we learned the history of Lourdes, where, back in the late 1800s, St. Bernadette saw apparitions of the Immaculate Conception. St. Bernadette was a fourteen-year-old girl who had respiratory problems and had eighteen visions of the Virgin Mary. It was in Lourdes that sixty-four miracles had been documented, and we were praying to be the sixty-fifth.

We got our miracle after the first evening of doing the nightly nine o'clock candlelight procession. Every night there was a crowd about 10,000 people from countries around the world. All the people had lit candles and were praying the rosary in their own languages. We were no different. Jena sat in her wheelchair while Ann, Al, Marc, Eric, and I began the mile-long procession. Halfway through, Eric started coughing and needed to sit for a while. Marc was ready to carry Jena when she said she would rather walk, and walk she did. She walked the entire procession, saying the rosary breathlessly. None of us could believe our eyes.

The next morning our itinerary had us doing the Stations of the Cross. The Stations of the Cross is a mile-long climb up the Mount of Espelugues, called Mount Calvary. It is a rough and steep climb that starts from the Upper Basilica. There are fifteen large stations, all with larger-than-life bronze statues illustrating the stages of Jesus' last days. Here you can walk in the path of Jesus on his last journey, and you can stop on the way to think and pray. They advised those in wheelchairs, the elderly, and those with any physical restrictions not to attempt the walk.

Jena once again disregarded warnings. Alan pushed an empty wheelchair up and down the mountain while Jena ran it. She walked or ran with Eric to each station of the lifelike statues. At each station, she stopped and prayed. She would look back at us every now and then with a knowing look. I never did quite understand those looks, but somehow Jena just seemed to belong there.

Our last stop before flying back home was the church of St. Gilard in Nevers, France. This is where St. Bernadette's body lies at rest in a glass tomb for all to see. Once again, we broke away from the tour and the six of us arrived in our van at the church just an hour before they closed for the day. When we got to the church, there was a Mass going on so we quietly sat in the back and listened. When the Mass ended, the priest turned off the lights and the church was lit only by a few candles. Jena had asked if she could kneel down in front of the altar to get a closer look at St. Bernadette, while the rest wanted to stroll around the grounds.

I stayed with Jena while she knelt down before the body of St. Bernadette. Jena did not move for twenty minutes. Then she slowly turned her head and looked at me with confusion. Her eyebrows were scrunched together as if she had been deep in thought and could not make sense of what she was thinking. She looked at me and said as though asking a question, "I know *her* like I know *you.*"

She looked at me for some sort of answer and when I had none, she slowly turned back and looked at St. Bernadette. It was a half hour later when the curator of the church said he was sorry but that he really needed to close down the church and we had to leave.

I was baffled by what Jena had said and she was quiet the whole ride back to the airport. Eric thought it was cool to see a real dead body out on display like that, and Alan said how lucky we were to have reached the church in time before our flight.

Jena didn't need oxygen during the ten-day trip, even though I insisted that she wear it at night. Jena didn't need oxygen on the flight home either. I had measured her oxygen levels throughout the trip and she had remained stable at her baseline the entire time. We thought we had received the miracle. I still believe we did.

On the airplane, Jena told me that St. Bernadette had visited her in her room many times and asked me if that made her crazy. I told her no. Just being a part of our family made her crazy; seeing St. Bernadette made her special. She liked that answer but asked me not to tell too many people because they might think she was especially crazy.

Chapter 14

After our return from France, Jena required more oxygen; her blood oxidation went from a baseline of 93 percent to 80, and sometimes 78 at night. Normal O_2 (oxidation) is 95-100. Anyone with a reading lower than that would normally be admitted to the hospital immediately. Jena's body had learned to compensate amazingly for the lower numbers. In addition to her four liters of oxygen, she had a bipap to wear at home, which she fought. Though the lack of oxygen was killing her slowly, Jena refused to wear the bipap.

Jena was evaluated in Pittsburgh, Pennsylvania, on October 24, 2006 for her double lung transplant. We were told that most likely it would be a three- to sixth-month wait for new lungs and another year or so until she was comfortable enough with the new set to go away on vacation. We realized that it would be at least two years before we could all go on another family trip. So now was the time to "make it happen." And we did.

I had been saving money for over three years so I could take Marc on a surprise fortieth birthday cruise. I had been planning a romantic twelve-day Mediterranean cruise, leaving from Barcelona, Spain, on November 1. After a five-minute discussion, we canceled our nonrefundable trip.

Jena was placed on the double lung transplant list at the thirty-sixth spot. A week later, we decided to take an RV trip to Florida—to Disney's Fort Wilderness, to be exact.

The day before we left, my mother called to offer her emotional support regarding Jena's double lung transplant. I was surprised, to say the least. Evidently, Evelyn had called her. My mother never called concerned about anyone other than herself. But I was still hoping that maybe, just maybe, she'd been lonely in her world long enough and had learned to care. All she kept saying was that she was offering her emotional support to me during this obviously hard time for me. Since she had been mostly absent from my life for twenty years, I questioned her about how she was giving me emotional support. She quickly said, "Apparently this was a mistake," and hung up.

The next day, we loaded up the RV and headed to the Flying J where we would stay on our way down to Florida. It was a great trip, yet a sad one all the same. It was here where we all realized how severe things were for Jena. She started wearing the bipap at night to assist in her breathing. She didn't have much reserve for anything and we limited our "fun" to just an hour or so each day. She was tired and wasn't able to do too much in addition to her routine of breathing treatments and sleeping.

Still, in Jena fashion, during that one hour a day she managed to drive a golf cart and go out to dinner, and she even drove a boat around Disney's Seven Sea Lagoon. Eric stood behind her as she drove, so he could jump in if she wanted a break. She wore her oxygen the whole time, except in any picture that I took of her, and she was even able to be our personal "guide." We had been in Disney World so often that she knew each hotel on the property by heart. As she drove the boat around the Seven Seas Lagoon, Jena lit up and giggled as we passed the Grand Floridian, where there was a young couple getting married.

She looked at me and then at Marc and smiled, *"You two lovebirds look like you want to get married, and you know you better hurry up because there is a seven-year waiting list to be married at the Grand Floridian—but it sure is worth the wait!"*

As we drove by the Polynesian Hotel, she took a breath and said, *"Ummm boy does that smell good! They have the best Luau on the east coast! The pork is to die for, but you might want to try their famous Mai Tai while you wait!"*

We smiled, and I took pictures of her. She kept us entertained the entire hour. She looked so happy. She was. She lived to the fullest when she could. She was amazing. We never did get to play minigolf, and I'm not sure I will ever want to again.

Chapter 15

Breathe

It was Tuesday, November 28, 2006. *The Today Show* was in our living room taping us for an upcoming segment on families with chronic diseases. Sabrina, the producer, and her crew from NBC had set up our house and we were all excited to be on TV. Jena wore her shiny red shirt, Eric was on the last week of a three-week course of IV antibiotics as a "tune-up," and I was doing last-minute cleaning to make sure everything was right. Jena had made us all decorate for Christmas over the weekend and the house looked festive, with the decorated tree and poinsettias all around. The NBC crew had moved everything in our living room to accommodate the lights and cameras.

Marc was talking with the camera guy when Jena said, "Are we really going to be on TV?" She was pale and her lips were bluer than normal. She had a mark on the bridge of her nose from the bipap she had been wearing, but she sat there smiling with excitement. Eric really didn't want to be on TV, especially because he was going through a tune-up. He didn't want people to know he had CF, and he certainly didn't want them to see him hooked up to an IV. But that is why NBC was here. Eric knew it was important, and he agreed to be a part of the segment.

When the crew left, early that evening, Jena said she was wiped out and wanted to go to bed. She climbed into bed about eight o'clock and said her lungs were sore, but she figured it was from all the coughing she had done that day. Jena slept propped up with pillows underneath her, and she said between that and the bipap, she felt a little better. I told her I would bring her to the hospital first thing in the morning and, without her usual argument, she agreed.

I fell asleep lying next to Jena, holding her until about 2 AM. Then I got up, brushed my teeth, and went to bed. I learned later that Marc had gotten up at 2:30 and had lain next to her the rest of the night.

Wednesday morning at 9 AM I called Dr. Boyer and said Jena needed to come in. Marc went to work and I told him I would call him once we got situated in the hospital. After all, we had been there fourteen times; Jena and I knew the routine. Eric would be home with his school tutor, Karryl, catching up on school work and said he was cool with it.

At 11:30 AM, I wheeled Jena into the admitting part of the emergency room at Westchester Medical Center in New York and started the paperwork. Jena sat there quietly. She was usually crabby and bossy when she was admitted to the hospital. She made the whole process very difficult, which was completely understandable. This time, however, she was helpful and understanding. It was almost like she knew something. Don, the nurse, told Jena that he had a bed waiting for her with her name on it whenever she was ready to move from her wheelchair to a more comfortable bed. After about ten minutes she told him she was ready and he wheeled in a bed with "Jena" written on it in black marker—a bed with her name on it. She smiled, and I started to cry.

People were just drawn to Jena, and Don was no exception. He started the normal procedure of starting an IV and taking a chest X-ray. It was at this moment that I heard the word *pneumothorax*. It was also the last time I knew the time and date. It was Wednesday, November 29, 2006 and it was 1:13

PM and I was in the emergency room at Maria Fareri Children's Hospital at Westchester Medical Center.

What do you say when you are told in the ER that you only have ten minutes to say everything you possibly can to your daughter? That's what I heard. A particular doctor—we'll call him Dr. Smarty-Pants—gave me just that scenario, which I look back on now as a gift.

Jena had had a pneumothorax. Here's a quick translation: Jena's lungs had filled with fluid and collapsed. The doctors were not able to get them reinflated. This is bad. Lungs are like balloons that stay "up," attached to a lining, if there is air or fluid in between the lungs and lining, they can collapse. Jena's lungs most likely collapsed while she was coughing because her airways were clogged with mucus.

In most instances, doctors can remove the air that caused the lungs to collapse and the lungs reinflate. In this case, they were able to remove the air, but the lungs would not stay up due to the scarring because of the bacteria that had caused infections and resulting lung damage. This is the devastation to the body that cystic fibrosis can cause.

The doctors told me that, because of this problem of severe lung damage, Jena's lungs were not able to convert oxygen properly. For those of us who slept in biology class, here's the CliffsNotes version: when we breathe in, we take in oxygen (O_2) from the air, and the lungs exchange that in the blood with carbon dioxide (CO_2), which is a waste gas that needs to get out. Too much CO_2 in the blood is bad. It's very bad.

Here's why. Too much CO_2 in you makes the body's natural pH balance decrease. That's bad. Quick short breaths now increase to compensate for the drop in pH. When your lungs are collapsed, breathing is beyond difficult, and the pH goes lower. When your pH is low, your kidneys are affected, and you go into kidney failure, and then your whole body shuts down. They have this very charming name for that in the hospital; they call it "crashing."

Dr. Smarty-Pants told me that if they didn't intubate Jena—meaning, put her on a ventilator to help her breathe, to help her exchange the oxygen—she would crash, and there would be nothing they could do to save her.

Once she was intubated, she would be unconscious. The only way we'd talk to her again would be after her double lung transplant, which would take place 500 miles away in Pittsburgh, Pennsylvania. As yet, there was no donor and we were still in New York.

Dr. Smarty-Pants gave me ten minutes.

Ten minutes.

That's all I get to tell Jena everything in my heart. To tell her how much joy she's brought me. To tell her how much I love her.

I had ten minutes.

I told her all those things. I told her that if I could be just a fraction of the person she was, I would be the most incredible person ever. I told her that if I could bring half of the smiles and laughter she did I would be honored to stand in her shadow the rest of my life. I cried. I couldn't stop crying.

As the tears relentlessly streamed down my face, I apologized for any and every fight we ever had. I apologized for any time she was mad at me or I was mad at her. I told her again and again how much I loved her, how proud I was of her, and how much she'd taught me that I would never be able to repay. I cried. I was shaking. I was terrified. I couldn't believe I was doing this, I couldn't believe that I *had* to.

Try to breathe.

She was wearing a bipap machine that covered her nose and mouth to help her breathe, but she was alert and awake and could talk to me. Jena, like a mother compassionately caring for her child, looked at me and gently shook her head left and right and slowly gave me the most remarkably tender smile. Her eyes looked so deeply into my eyes, like never before. It felt as though she was reaching into my soul with her eyes, and I could feel it. I looked back at her with my bloodshot eyes, sniffling, and my hands shaking in hers.

Jena just said, "Mommy, I *love* you."

There were no tears in her eyes, and there was no fear either; no screaming, no asking why her. Jena in her infinite wisdom knew that love is the greatest of all. All this chaos was inconsequential. Love is what is immortal. Her love for me and mine for her were untouchable. Jena knew love is the only answer. Now I know that, too.

God must have been touched at that moment because Jena's blood gases stabilized enough for her pulmonologist, Dr. B., to convince Dr. Smarty-Pants that Jena was a fighter and that her body could compensate enough to get her to the Pediatric Intensive Care Unit (PICU), which was on the second floor. Dr. B. also thought perhaps Jena's strength might get her to Pittsburgh, though we all knew he could not make any such promises. He gravely told us that the decisions we made we would have to live with. He told us there would be no "Monday morning quarterbacking." I prayed to God and looked at Jena. I knew she was a fighter and she would make it to Pittsburgh. Dr. Smarty-Pants didn't know who he was up against.

With seven doctors and four nurses, in unison, wheeling machines, tubes, and Jena, we were able to get her to the PICU on the second floor in fifty-two seconds.

Jena always seemed to know what really mattered in this world, and what mattered was not getting to live longer, but the love you give while you're here. She gave me a lifetime of love.

Chapter 16

Just step over me, I thought.

I just wanted Marc to step over me and leave me here. I was a terrible mother. I was on the floor with no shoes or socks, my hair was wet, and I couldn't move. We were supposed to be on the med flight to Pittsburgh with Jena in forty-five minutes. I had tried to take a shower while Marc stayed with Jena in the PICU with Dr. B., and here I was on the floor at the Ronald McDonald House at Westchester Medical Center.

Since yesterday I hadn't eaten, I hadn't slept, I couldn't stop throwing up, I had diarrhea and a migraine, and my blood pressure was through the roof. And there I lay on the floor as the manager of the Ronald McDonald House stood at my feet. She had no idea what to do with me and kept reminding me to relax and put my feet up and breathe.

Relax?

Breathe?

I should have been with Jena, but I couldn't even sit up. To relax and put my feet up and breathe sounded so ludicrous while my entire world was falling apart, yet it was the only thing I was able to do. I told the nice lady to please call Madelint immediately, since she'd know what to do, and I gave her Madelint's number, which I knew by heart.

Madelint was my lifesaver and my friend, and she also happened to be Dr. Boyer's right arm. She was a registered nurse with a master's degree in social work, and, over the years, I am sure that degree had come in handy more than once in dealing with me. She always popped her head in every time we were in the hospital, or at a doctor's appointment; even if it wasn't with Dr. B., she'd be there. She was wonderful, and she was the only person who could help me. She would know exactly what to do.

She had been with me all day the day before in the ER while they attempted to reinflate Jena's collapsed lungs. She was there to hold my hand and just to be there.

In a matter of minutes, she was beside me again. She brought with her another nurse and Dr. B. They knew what was going on, and they knew I had to be on that plane to Pittsburgh or I would never be able to live with myself. They all got on the floor with me, checked my temperature, checked my pulse, checked my heart rate, and held my hand. I knew they would take care of me. Dr. B. said I needed Valium, and I would be fine. Even in the state I was in, I didn't think that was such a good idea. The last thing I wanted to be was knocked out. I had to be here for Jena, but I was no good to anyone on the floor.

"Just step over me and take care of Jena!" I cried.

Dr. B. just grinned knowingly and told Madelint to take me through the ER and do it *now*. He was going back to be with Jena and Marc. They should have just stepped over me, but I owe them everything that they didn't.

Madelint helped me into a wheelchair. I was so dizzy I didn't know we were already in the ER, where she signed me in, answered all the questions, and asked them to please hurry. The woman in admissions asked if she was my mother, and I answered, "I wish."

In fifteen minutes I had been diagnosed with severe anxiety, panic attack, and trauma. The ER doctor on call prescribed me five milligrams of Valium with five refill prescriptions. Madelint had explained what was going on with Jena, and he figured I might need more. Unfortunately, both he and Dr. B. were right. Within five minutes of taking the Valium, all my symptoms subsided to a bearable level, I could function again, and my first thought was Jena.

I had to get to her. What if I was too late for the flight, and they had left without me?

Just as I stood up and was ready to run upstairs, my closest and dearest friends, Cindy, Jo-Ann, and Tara, walked in. I had called Tara on my cell phone the day before while Jena was in surgery and asked her to pray. I had asked her to ask everyone to pray. I knew this wasn't good.

We made it down to Jena's room, and soon I was holding her hand and telling her how sorry I was to have been gone so long. Jena smiled as she scolded me with her finger and waved "hi" to everyone. They all took turns giving her a kiss and trying to hold back their tears.

I turned around to see three people dressed in red flight suits walk into the room. They were here. We would be leaving for Pittsburgh in minutes; I had just made it in time. They told us that they had a small plane, and only one parent would fit on the plane. Marc said I should go with Jena, and he would drive out there in our car.

"Hang on a minute ..." Tara's husband, Tim, interrupted Marc's plan.

"... you both have been up for two days and she's drugged up and you're exhausted. What happens when Margarete crashes while she's with Jena, and you fall asleep at the wheel? Neither one of you is in any condition to handle that." He pointed to Marc. "Why don't you go with Jena in the plane, and I'll drive her out there right behind you?"

Tim's plan made sense. That's why you want friends you trust around you to help you when you're not thinking clearly—and neither one of us was.

"How much do you two weigh?" asked the tall guy in the red flight suit.

"315 together," Marc answered.

I couldn't add one plus one at this point, yet it was no surprise to me that Marc could compute figures without missing a beat. "She's 135 and I'm 180."

"You can both go, but neither of you can go in the ambulance; you'll have to follow us to the airport," the guy in the red suit added.

I was so relieved to know we would all be able to go together. Jena clapped her hands and gave thumbs up. It was getting hard for her to talk, between the bipap and recovering from the two surgeries, so she and I made hand signals to communicate. We always came up with something. I hugged Tara, Jo-Ann, and Cindy good-bye, and they kissed Jena.

Tim drove us in our car to the airport. He was so close behind the ambulance I could see Jena through the back window. He wasn't going to lose the ambulance no matter how fast it was going or how many red lights it went through. Rules don't matter much to Tim, friends do, and he was there to get us to where we needed to be. The coincidence of how it all worked was unbelievable; it couldn't have been timed any better.

Chapter 17

Our car, Tim at the wheel, followed the ambulance into the restricted area at the local airport. The guy in the red flight suit wheeled Jena out of the ambulance on a gurney and pushed her toward the tiny plane. Marc and I were already inside the plane when Jena gave Tim the thumbs up as they lifted her into the doorway hatch. We were on our way to Pittsburgh *without* Jena being intubated. Take that, Dr. Smarty-Pants.

Either it was the Valium in me, or I just knew we would make it to Pittsburgh, because I didn't seem nearly as distressed as Marc was. He asked the guy in the red flight suit, "Are you sure that's enough oxygen?"

We would be in Pittsburgh in two hours. Or so we thought. During the flight, the woman in the red flight suit kept calling up to the pilot and asking how much farther. She must not have liked the answer because she informed him that they needed to make an emergency stop. We were running out of oxygen, and they needed to get a helicopter ready to take us directly to the hospital. Jena didn't have time for an ambulance.

We landed, and they exchanged two more large oxygen tanks. We hoped that this time it would be enough. Each takeoff and landing was especially hard on Jena. Her pain medication was starting to wear off. The lady in the red suit called ahead to have more IV pain medicine waiting for us on the rooftop of the hospital.

Fifteen minutes after we resumed our flight, Jena's bipap machine went dead. The battery had died. The woman in the red flight suit said they would attach it to the plane and go on auxiliary. She took out a plug and connected it to the plane. Nothing happened. She looked at the other guy, and he immediately dumped out a large duffle bag full of cords and plugs. He tried plug after plug while the third guy in the red flight suit took care of Jena. Her numbers were dropping quickly. He manually squeezed a bag that was also attached to the oxygen tank to help her breathe. There was nothing we could do but watch this unravel.

If it weren't for the Valium, I might have been throwing up at this point, or passed out on the floor. Mercifully, I was still holding my own, but Marc wasn't faring too well. He was pale and shaking, and he looked like he could kill someone with his bare hands. It had been the guy in the red flight suit who had smiled and said "yes" when Marc asked in New York if he had enough oxygen for the flight.

The two of them were still scrambling with plugs until finally, after fifty seconds of sheer terror, the last plug fit and the machine kicked on. Jena's numbers were going back up and we were back in action.

After a few minutes, Marc started to get color back in his face, and he was now trying to get his own breathing under control. Jena was worn down, and you could hear her moaning over the roar of the engine and her now-working bipap machine. She needed the IV pain medicine, and the Valium I took back in New York was rapidly wearing off.

The flight, which should have taken two hours, had taken four. Mercifully, the helicopter that would take us to Children's Hospital was ready for takeoff. I went with Jena in the helicopter while Marc went with the man in the red suit. The helicopter pilot asked me if I was OK. I told him I had a terrible fear of heights. He said he did too and that I would be fine and then he gave me a thumbs up. I took in a deep breath, gave him thumbs up, and looked back at Jena, who was already giving her thumbs up. That was my girl. She was so brave; I was the one who was terrified, not about the flight, but that there was nothing I could do. All I could think of was getting her stable as fast as possible.

We made it from the airport in Pittsburgh to the Children's Hospital in seven minutes. A nurse and a doctor were already waiting on the rooftop when we arrived. I told the nurse that Jena was in pain, and she pulled a small syringe out of her left pocket. She noticed then that it had accidentally been pushed already and announced that she would have to get another one. I think I could have killed her right there without blinking. She must have noticed my expression because she hurriedly radioed ahead to the PICU, asking that they have the medicine waiting for us. We raced through hallways and elevators almost as fast as we had in New York. We arrived in the PICU, and the syringe and Marc were both there waiting for Jena.

Jena was resting comfortably now. They had hooked her up to ten IV pumps, a bipap machine, and two monitoring machines. Hours went by, and then they asked me to go downstairs and sign in; I would need a pass for the hospital. A medical student brought me downstairs to the front desk and then disappeared. It must have been morning; I could see light coming through the front window.

"Please sign in. First and last name, date and time, where you parked with the parking pass, and what room you are visiting," said the gentleman behind the counter, never lifting his head from his newspaper as he sipped his coffee.

"My name is Margarete Cassalina; I came in from the roof last night. I don't know what time it is. I don't know what day it is. I don't know what room or floor my daughter is on, and I was told I need a pass."

The gentleman looked up from his paper and put his coffee down. His face softened as he walked around the counter toward me.

"Don't worry, sweetheart. I'll help you."

Chapter 18

Timing is everything. Most of the time you can't plan the perfect "time" no matter how hard you try, and life seems to have a plan all its own, anyway. Marc and I never planned the perfect time to have a family; we were just thankful for the one we had. We didn't plan for our kids to have CF, yet they did, and we made time to live. We never planned to be told we had ten minutes left with our daughter and then find we had more time.

Once we arrived in Pittsburgh, time had become everything. Every second counted, every breath was celebrated. Time was ticking so loudly at this point it was deafening. It was no more than five minutes after they took yet another blood gas sample from Jena's central line that the doctor from the PICU returned. He grasped in his hand a tiny handheld machine. That tiny machine would dictate the future of my daughter. What the numbers read would determine where we went from there. The number read 132. That's not the number we were looking for. It was the highest number the machine could register.

Once again, Jena had pushed the limits, but this time it was not in her favor. Jena's lungs had had enough. Her CO_2 had reached critical levels, and her pH balance was dropping. We knew they could wait no longer to put her on a respirator. They needed to intubate her. We had been pushing this off for two days; now push came to shove, and we had nothing left to use. There were no new lungs in sight for her, and intubation was our only option.

Ding.
The timer was up.

By the look on his face, the PICU doctor's heart was broken too. He had fought right alongside Jena and had been captivated by her smile. Her internal fight and love of life captured everyone; no one was safe from her addictive smile and her unshakable determination. The doctor looked at us, closed his eyes for a moment, and let out a heavy sigh, sadly and knowingly. He had been down this road before, and it was a road he would rather not travel.

As he explained the procedure to us, Jena's nurse brought in a red bag with the word *Intubation* written across the middle in bold letters. She didn't say a word. She couldn't even look at us.

In Jena's condition, being intubated meant she had approximately one week to get a gift of new lungs or she would not live. Being intubated gave her a finite length of time. Her lungs were completely done, and it was only a matter of time until the rest of her body followed. Intubation means there is no more "Jena fight" in Jena. They also had to put her in a medically induced coma so she didn't have to fight all that was being done to her body. All this medical science was buying her time, but without Jena in the fight, science didn't have a chance.

I can't breathe anymore

My strength ended at the sight of that word, *Intubation*. I stopped listening to the doctor, walked numbly past the nurse, and got as close to Jena as I could. Jena, at this point, was unconscious. I was not sure she could hear me or even know that I was there. Still, I stroked her matted hair, kissed her all over her salty face again and again and again. It was eerily reminiscent of the emergency room back in New York. I told her how much I loved her. I told her how proud I was to be her mother. I shook, I cried, I kissed her all over her face, arms, hands, and even her toes. This time, Jena was not looking back at me. This time there was no response from her. I could hear my heart breaking. I took a long look at my beautiful thirteen-year-old daughter. I could barely see her through my tears. I didn't think I was breathing anymore. Mechanically, I hit the large blue button next to the exit door. The doors opened up automatically. I couldn't look back. I couldn't stay. I couldn't even be. I left Marc to survive this torment alone. I couldn't help him.

I was barely breathing as I took out my cell phone. I called my in-laws, Ann and Al, who had left the hospital not thirty minutes earlier to go back to the hotel. I couldn't even get out a complete sentence. Through my gasps I managed to say, "In ... tu ... bation ... now."

I hung up and looked up at the ceiling as if God Himself were there. I didn't say a word. I couldn't. I thought to myself and screamed in my head, "*I can't do this!*" It was 12:45 AM. I hadn't slept more than an hour here or there in days. I hadn't eaten, either. I didn't care if I ever did again.

"I can't do this!"

Just at that moment the elevator doors opened and out walked my friends Cindy and Jo-Ann and their husbands David and Bob. I looked again because I thought I was seeing things.

I hadn't spoken to them since I saw them in the PICU in New York. Somehow they were there, too. How could they be *here* in Pittsburgh? How could they be here *now, right at this very second?* Right when I needed them the most? Cindy looked at me and must not have liked what she saw; her eyes widened and she looked scared.

She screamed, "*What?*"

I stamped my feet in defiance and yelled, "Don't do that!"

She took a step closer to me, and I collapsed on the floor. I had nothing left in me. I was in shock about Jena; I was in shock that my dearest friends were there at a time when I needed them more than ever.

By now, Marc was walking around the corner. His eyes were puffy and red. He did a double take, received a hug from David, and tried to hold back his pain. Marc is the strongest man I've even known. Somehow he was able to tell them the news; I was barely conscious. By the time Marc was done, my in-laws had arrived. We were all exhausted and numb. Jo-Ann and Cindy helped me off the floor and we all walked into the PICU waiting room.

I started to sip my water as the doctor walked in. He told us that Jena was on the respirator and that she was stable. He told us that we could go and see Jena. I knew that was something I couldn't do. Marc stood up, let out a heavy sigh, and looked at the ground, covering his face with both hands so he could pull himself together. Ann and Al got up, too. Alan put his hand on Marc's shoulder and gave a squeeze. It was his way of letting Marc know that he was there for him. Ann was crying as she kept walking slowly in the direction none of them wanted to go. But that's where Jena was, so they kept going.

Cindy and Jo-Ann and David and Bob stayed with us in the Pediatric Intensive Care Unit waiting room for two days. They checked into a nearby hotel but never stayed there. They slept sitting up in chairs or curled up in the corner on the floor, using a coat as a blanket. They never left my side. They brought me food that I never ate, they brought me coffee that got cold, and they brought me pillows I didn't use. I couldn't have made it through without all that they gave. They gave all they had, just like Jena. I realized that their being there was all I could possibly need. Sometimes the best thing to say is nothing, and the best thing to do is just to be there. And they were.

Chapter 19

Twenty-four hours after the intubation, Jena went into cardiac arrest. That morning I had been rubbing her feet and arms while we played her iPod in her ears. I hoped that if she could still hear, she could listen to her music instead of the horrible sounds of the hospital machines. I had been praying incessantly. My prayers had turned to rage. I prayed fast, I prayed hard, I prayed in anger. I thought if I prayed long enough, said the right prayers, and concentrated hard enough that she would be OK, that God would make everything OK. Isn't that what prayer is for? He'd come through, after all. I had such strong faith.

Breathe

At some point during my prayers, I noticed that all the numbers on the hospital machines were dropping, and Jena was crashing; so did her nurse. That word "crashing"—the word Dr. Smarty-Pants had warned me about. Jena, attached to fourteen machines and on a respirator, was crashing. The head of the PICU unit came rushing in with a team of doctors to work on Jena while the nurse cleared the unit of all visitors except for me and Marc. We found ourselves with no strength to stand, curled together on the floor ten feet away from Jena watching the whole nightmare unfold. These doctors knew what they were doing. They used every ounce of what they knew to get Jena back.

Breathe

I felt the cold floor underneath me and Marc's arms holding me. I don't know which one of us was trembling. I prayed to God, I prayed to Jena. I might have been hallucinating at this time, but I heard Jena's voice tell me it was time for her to go home; she wanted to go and it was OK. She also told me that I shouldn't pray that way, prayer is not meant to be said in anger or rage—that's not what prayer is for, that prayer is a gift, a conversation, not a bartering tool. I told her I loved her, and I would always love her, and I told her to do what she needed to do, that I'd let her go. And I promised to pray the right way from then on.

The doctors in Pittsburgh were phenomenal, and Jena was stabilized once again. But now she had a fever and her eyes were not dilating properly. This was bad. They needed to call in a neurologist to measure her brainwave activity, and they needed to put her on a cooling blanket to bring down her fever. I knew Jena was doing all of this for Marc. He needed to make sure every *t* was crossed, and every *i* was dotted, and everything medically possible was done, so there would be no regrets. He would never be able to move forward if he thought for a moment that he hadn't done everything possible to save his little girl. He didn't recognize that his being her father was all she ever needed. This I know for sure. As for me, I had let her go on the cold cement floor of the PICU the day before.

Breathe

We never left her side while my in-laws came in and out of the room. By now my sister, Evelyn, had arrived from New York, and so had Mike, with his girlfriend, Mary. Marc and I knew it was time for Eric to come. It might be the last time he would be able to see his sister. He was home in New York with Marc's sister, Lisa. She and John B., Marc's cousin and the best man at our wedding, brought Eric to Pittsburgh in record time.

Breathe

At 3 AM Monday morning everyone was sleeping, whether it was in a chair, on the floor or at the hotel—everyone except Marc and I. We were in with Jena while they were bringing down her fever and putting electrodes on her head to measure brain activity. It was certain that her brain functions had deteriorated, and they anticipated that by morning, after another reevaluation, her brain function would be minimal.

Breathe

Jena had suffered severe brain damage. There would be no coming out of this; there would be no way for Jena to come back as Jena anymore. She had left nothing to doubt, nothing to regret, nothing more medically possible to be done. I sat in the chair, holding her hand, knowing she was leaving us, and began to pray. "Now I lay you down to sleep, I pray the Lord your soul to keep. Should you die before you wake, I pray the Lord your soul to take."

Marc looked at me, baffled. I looked back at Jena and started the prayer again. Marc reached for my other hand and joined me.

"Now I lay you down to sleep, I pray the Lord your soul to keep. Should you die before you wake, I pray the Lord your soul to take."

At that moment we both felt a rush in the room. The energy felt so strong, like a fan blowing from the floor without any wind. I felt tingling throughout my body, and I felt peace in my heart. I knew in that moment Jena had left her body and would be with Him whom she saw; Him whom she told us was there. I knew she was leaving us, but she waited for me to tell her it was OK to go, she waited for her daddy to get what he so desperately needed so he would now be able to move forward in life, and she waited until her brother arrived to say good-bye. She orchestrated it beautifully, making sure we had enough emotional support to get us through each breath. I told you she was amazing.

Breathe

The second-to-last sentence that Jena ever spoke right before she was intubated was, "*I can't see but I'm not blind.*" She said this three times. Then she said, "*I can see Him and you can't. Tell them.*" She said this three times, with a smile and purpose.

Breathe

She never said another word.

Breathe

One thing I know for sure is what she meant. I know whom she saw and what she was saying.

Breathe

I know that all the successes in this world pale in comparison to the gift I got that night. I know my baby girl had met God face-to-face that day, and that outshines any of this world's accomplishments. To get your child to heaven is, in my book, the greatest success a parent can possibly achieve. He Himself came to take her home.

Breathe

One thing I know for sure is that I will see Jena again.

Breathe

At 3:13 AM I got up from my chair, gave Jena a "Jena kiss" which is three quick kisses on one cheek, then the other cheek, then the forehead, and one kiss on the nose. I whispered, "I love you JJ" in her ear, wiped the tears from my eyes, and walked back to the PICU waiting room to let everyone know it would be a matter of hours.

Breathe

Marc stayed with Jena the entire time.

Breathe

Ann, Alan, Lisa, and John all arrived and went in with Jena and Marc, all waiting for the machines to tell us what we already knew.

Breathe

I stayed with Eric while the rest arrived.

Breathe

I held Eric in my arms, and we talked.

Breathe

He wanted to go see her but didn't want to remember her attached to machines, wires, tubes; she was never made for that.

Breathe

I told Eric that was fine and to do what he felt he could handle.

Breathe
Breathe
Breathe ...
At 9:57 AM Jena's body was done with suffering.

Chapter 20

Everyone in the PICU waiting room was silent; the only sounds were sniffles and moans.

The room stayed quiet until Eric said softly, with tears rolling down his cheeks, "Isn't it ironic how we have to suffer because Jena's not, and we have to be sad because Jena's happy?"

Eric is pretty amazing, too.

"What was Jena's favorite candy?"

Odd question coming from a hospital pastor at 11 AM in the morning. It was an odd way to console us.

"Peppermint Patties," I answered in bewilderment at his question. I didn't realize I had a little smile on my face, thinking about how much she loved to eat them one after another. I pulled another tissue out of the box and threw the saturated ones in the basket. I gave the box back to Eric.

The pastor continued, "I lost my brother twelve years ago and not a day goes by that I don't cry about him. He liked Snickers bars."

Maybe I was exhausted, maybe I was in shock, but I was extremely confused by the conversation we were having with this hospital pastor.

"When I think of Snickers, I think of my brother. What do you do when you get a candy bar?" he asked, not really wanting an answer.

Now I know I was disoriented, but this was just not making any sense. He was talking directly to Eric. The pastor's voice was deep and soothing and somehow I trusted him, and I let him continue.

"You throw away the wrapper to get to the good stuff, right? Well, I think of my brother as the good stuff, the candy. What it's made of, not

61

what contains it. The wrapper is just the shell of the good stuff. The wrapper can get ripped, torn, crumpled, but the candy is always the perfect part. My brother's wrapper is gone, but the good stuff is in me. And when I see a Snickers bar, I think of him."

I got it; the light bulb went off in my foggy head. Jena's soul is the patty and the wrapper is her body, her skin. I'd never conceived of a peppermint patty like that. Why would I have? Then I began to analyze it a little more. Its silver-blue foil wrapper is made fairly durable; it can withstand a lot of damage and still protect the inner mint patty. And then there is the yummy chocolate part; it's refreshing, it's sweet and small, always leaving you wanting more. It also happens to be shaped like the host you get at church. No wonder Jena's favorite candy was a Peppermint Patty. No wonder they handed out over 1,200 Peppermint Patties at her funeral. No wonder I placed a Peppermint Patty wrapper in her coffin before they closed it. No wonder I still cry every time I see a Peppermint Patty.

I know I will see her again. I know prayer keeps us together. In the meantime, I will enjoy her energy, which is around me always; the gifts she leaves me; a smell, a song, a sign, or a penny found somewhere least expected. That's my Jena.

Chapter 21

December 9, 2006, was the day of Jena's funeral. Our little local St. James Church usually holds about 400 people on a good day; that morning it exceeded capacity by threefold. There wasn't an empty space to be found, and even though it was a brisk winter's morning, there were still more people standing outside throughout the entire Mass because they needed to be there. Peppermint Patties were handed out to everyone that day in honor of Jena, and they ran out at 1,200 candies.

That Saturday morning, St. James was filled with Catholics, Protestants, and Jews. It was filled with people who had never been to a Catholic church and some who go every day. It was filled with those who believe in God and those who don't. The thing that brought all of them together was Jena. Through God's grace, my daughter once again touched people to the core.

I had asked my friends to make sure Dr. B. sat up at the front at the funeral Mass. Dr. Boyer had been Eric and Jena's pulmonologist for thirteen years after Dr. Kanengiser left for private practice in New Jersey. Dr. K. diagnosed the kids, but Dr. B. saw them grow.

Dr. Boyer has been there for it all. He sat on Jena's tiny red tricycle for two hours, taking tape off a very frightened little two-year-old girl's IV, which was no longer working, because she wouldn't let anyone else come near her. He stayed in the hospital after hours, making sure that the kids were brought down to get their tests and X-rays done, or else he would bring them there himself. He'd stay late, sitting in the visitor's chair, explaining in depth what latest complication had occurred, and he always made sure that Jena's room was cold, just the way she liked it.

"Make it like a meat locker in here," he would call from her room phone down to hospital maintenance, giving her a wink and a smile.

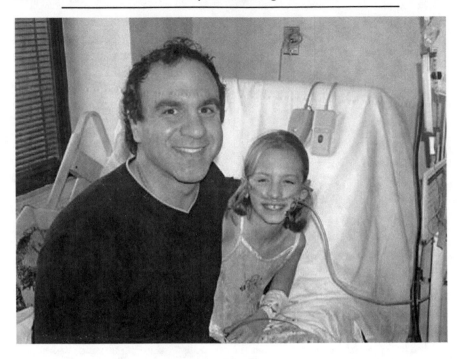

He did this even though his family was waiting for him at home. He is aggressive when dealing with the destructive evils of CF; he is optimistic and compassionate about the importance of living. Dr. B. is straightforward and a fantastic doctor. We are indebted to him that we had Jena as long as we did, and we are grateful that he is taking care of Eric. He is family to us, and we wanted him to know it.

My friends took good care of Dr. B. that day. They made sure he sat in the front pew; they made sure he knew where the cemetery was, and they made sure he made it to St. Mary's Hall afterward as well. They made him a plate big enough for two people to eat and sat him at their table. They asked him medical questions and personal questions, and they told him how sorry they were about Jena. They knew he had lost her, as well. She was his girl, too; he'd watched her grow, and he knew her literally from the inside out. He knew how much she'd struggled, and he also knew how determined she was. Now he knew the community she'd grown up in, and how blessed we are to live here.

I think my father saw that, too. Standing next to me with his wife Sherry for the two-day wake, where he met 2,000 strangers, and being at the overcrowded funeral, I think my father understood for the first time the choices I had made, the community where I lived, and the friends that I have. I think for the first time he was proud of the person I had grown up to be.

I think he was sad how much he had missed. It was great to have him there with me, standing next to me, just being there with me.

My mother, on the other hand, was true to form: glaringly absent.

Mike, Marc's business partner and friend for over twenty years, sat in the pew across from us. Jena had touched Mike to the core. Mike is one of the funniest people I know and can find humor in almost anything, but not that day. He is also not a church-going guy; but he was that day.

I looked over at him and saw that his eyes were swollen and red, and he wasn't hiding the tears streaming down his face. Our eyes met and he mouthed to me "thank you" and looked back at the small white coffin at the front of the church. I knew he meant how thankful he was to have known Jena, to be included in our lives like family, and thankful that he knew our Jena kind of love. I saw Mike reach for Mary's hand, which was clutching a tissue. Mary looked up at Mike, squeezed his hand, and then rested her head on his shoulder. They were both crying. Jena had loved Mike and Mary in a very special way, and they loved her. Unicorns will always be their private joke, which will bring him to tears. Mike was touched by a little girl who could make him laugh and show him love. He is forever changed. He was also one of the strongest souls who carried her out of the church that day. I don't know how he did it.

That cold morning in Milton, people overcame their differences and joined together in love and grief. If only the world could understand truth like that of a child's purpose.

Chapter 22

So faith, hope, love remain, these three;
But the greatest of these is love.

−1 Corinthians 13

December 5, 2006

Jena Marie Cassalina

An Angel has ascended back to Heaven, Jena Marie Cassalina entered into God's Loving Hands on Monday, December 4, 2006 at Pittsburgh's Children's Hospital. Jena was surrounded by her loving parents Marc and Margarete, her loving brother Eric and her loving Grandparents, Aunts, Cousins and Dear Friends

Jena age 13 was born March 13, 1993 at Vassar Hospital in Poughkeepsie; she was an eighth grade student at the Marlboro Middle School and a member of St. James Church in Milton. Jena was a special gift from God. She radiated light, hope and faith from her beautiful smile. Jena enjoyed her life while courageously fighting her battle against Cystic Fibrosis. She was an avid reader, loved to travel and could debate any topic with poise beyond her years. She impacted so many people in her short life; Jena's greatest wish was to have CF stand for Cure Found, for her brother Eric and all others still in the fight. Jena's last contribution to win the battle was to donate her lungs to continue the research for a cure. In lieu of flowers The Cassalina Family and Jena ask that anyone please make donations to The Cystic Fibrosis Foundation and mail them to the family.

Jena is survived by her loving parents Marc and Margarete McCord Cassalina, and her beloved big brother Eric Cassalina, of Milton NY. Her Paternal Grandparents are Alan and Ann Cassalina of Milton, Her Maternal Grandparents Bill and Sherry McCord of Florida. She is survived by three of her Great-grandmothers, Grandma Helen Marcello of Florida, Oma Eva Spingola of Florida and Oma Martha McCord of Plattsburgh NY. She is also survived by her Aunt Lisa and Dominick Rosso of Milton. Her Aunt Evelyn Keable of Plattsburgh and Uncle Matthew McCord of Florida and Uncle John Keable of Plattsburgh. First Cousins, Ashley, Giavanna, and Dominick Rosso, Anna, Alicia and Jonathan Keable.

Visitation will be held on Thursday Dec 7, 6-8pm, Friday Dec 8, 2-4 & 6-9 at The DiDonato Funeral Home 1290 Route 9W Marlboro NY. A Mass of Christian Burial will be held Saturday Dec 9, 11:00 am at St James Roman Catholic Church in Milton with the Most Reverend Bishop Dominick J. Lagonegro and the Reverend Fred Kempfirl officiating.

Jena will be laid to rest at St. Mary's Cemetery in Marlboro

Jena was a rose in the garden of life.

Arrangements by The DiDonato Funeral Service, Inc., Carl J. DiDonato, Jr. and Lawrence M. Cavazza 1290 Route 9W, Marlboro, NY 12542 (845) 236-4300

Chapter 23

We had no idea that Jena's obituary would be shared with as many as it was, and that it would touch over 2,000 people, who expressed their condolences in person during a two-day wake. We had no idea of the magnitude of her effect on people, but I am sure that she did.

Every night after the funeral, with a few tissue boxes on hand, Eric, Marc, and I would go through every single card and letter that was sent to us and read each one out loud. It was our way of honoring Jena and the person who had been moved to write us. Almost every card contained a donation to fight CF and in every one was a handwritten note to us. We received 1,135 letters in two weeks. Those 1,135 letters contained $73,436.00 and we thanked the sender of every one of them.

We received many cards and letters from complete strangers that began:

> "… I have never met you or your family, but your story and
> your daughter have touched me in a way I can't explain …"

We have heard stories from families who have reunited after decades of not speaking because something inside them was touched by knowing Jena. The following was the Bishop Dunn Memorial newsletter, written by the school's principal, Mr. DelViscio, that went out to the school:

> "The highest tribute to those who have died is not grief but
> gratitude."-Thornton Wilder

December 2006

Dear Parents/Guardians, Students and Friends of Bishop Dunn,

We have been very fortunate these past few years. Many of us at Bishop Dunn have had the privilege of getting to know **Jena Cassalina**, a sweet, strong, special angel in a fragile little girl's disguise, who passed away Monday of complications stemming from a lifelong battle with Cystic Fibrosis. Those who have been touched by Jena are also very lucky to have received a very precious gift from her before she left us. The gift is the memory of an infectious smile, unforgettable laugh and iron-strong will that I, for one, will carry with me for the rest of my life and call to mind whenever I am faced with some difficulty that I don't know how to handle.

It is so easy to hold onto that happy, smiling, positive image of her because that is how she always acted when she was with us as a student in 5th, 6th and 7th grade. Despite her always bright and enthusiastic approach to life, we knew that she suffered - from being poked and probed constantly, from reactions to the dozens of medications that she had to take to try and keep her affliction at bay, from the lung-clearing procedures that had to be performed almost every day to allow her simply to breathe on her own. But she never let any of the suffering come through or dampen her spirits – at least not in front of us.

She could have complained, but she didn't. We would have understood if she had been miserable and depressed, but she wasn't. Lord knows, she might have given up a long time ago, and we wouldn't have thought less of her. I didn't have the privilege to be with her in the end, but I have no doubt that she never did give up in spirit or in heart. The only thing that she couldn't control, her body, simply wouldn't cooperate anymore.

It is amazing how much impact one person can have on so many in 13 short years of life, and while I am very sad for all those who have been touched by her, especially her family, I am glad that she can breathe freely again without the burden of a decaying body weighing her down in that place we call heaven. It's in that place now with God and all the other angels, where I imagine Jena has already begun captivating everyone, as she did here, with her infectious smile and unforgettable laugh.

At the beginning of the sermon at Jena Cassalina's Funeral Mass Saturday, it was suggested that all those who had been touched by this physically fragile but spiritually strong little girl "would have gladly traded all their memories of her just to have her back." The problem is that I doubt that Jena would have wanted to come back if it meant erasing all of the beautiful memories that she had helped create in her very short but immeasurably fulfilling life here on earth.

In fact, as I looked around me at the hundreds of friends and family filling to twice its capacity the tiny church in Milton where she was baptized, confirmed and finally blessed, praised and prayed over before departing for heaven, the more I came to be convinced that this was why Jena was put on earth – to leave all those lucky enough to have known her with wonderful, powerful memories of laughter in the face of unremitting pain, hope demonstrated where most others might not believe it could exist, and, most importantly, memories of how faith in God and love for others can make it possible to gladly bear the most difficult of life's burdens.

At the end of Saturday's moving ceremony, I was sad but also strangely elated that Jena had been so successful in accomplishing God's mission for her by showing everyone who has shared any time with her how each moment of life, no matter how short, should be savored even when we are weighed down by suffering. As she was carried out of the church, while a choir of her girlhood friends sang over and over again the moving and soulful refrain, "Let it breathe on me, let it breathe on me, let the breath of God breathe on me," a simple, but even more profound thought struck me. Jena wasn't just sent by God, she WAS the breath of God. And we are all more blessed today for her having breathed on us."

Three weeks after Jena's passing, Principal DelViscio received this letter.

January 29th, 2007

Dear Mr. DelViscio,

Several times during the past month, I have wanted to share these thoughts with you, but found myself choking back tears before I could even begin. I have decided it might present itself better in a letter.

Most importantly, I want to thank you and Bishop Dunn Memorial School staff for including our friend, Matthew and his family in your prayers. Matthew, 11 years old, died tragically after being hit by a car in early December. It happened to be the same week that BDMS lost one of their own, Jena Cassalina.

During this sad time, it was a comfort to know the "Bishop Dunn family" not only mourned and prayed for Jena , but also reached out in prayer to our friends. This show of love was felt deeply. It was a comfort to know that my daughter AmyBeth was surrounded by compassion and spiritual strength at school while she dealt with the sadness of losing two friends in the same week.

While you may have heard some of what follows through Father Bill or some of AmyBeth's teachers, I wanted to relay it to you myself. While tragic, it seems a story meant to be shared. It is a story of the tragedy of death, but within it lies a story of the beauty of the gift of life through organ donation.

After receiving a call from BDMS notifying me of Jena's passing, I spoke with my good friend and neighbor, Robin. She detected sadness in my voice and I told her AmyBeth's friend had passed. During our conversation, I mentioned Jena had been on a list awaiting a lung transplant. As mothers, Robin and my heartfelt thoughts words and thoughts were of Jena's parents. We spoke of how painful it must be to lose a child. We mentioned how precious each moment shared with a loved one is. We also spoke about organ donation. I told her Jena had requested to donate her lung for cystic fibrosis research.

A half hour after Robin and I had this conversation, I was called to the scene of an accident. Robin's son, Matthew, had been hit by a car while riding his bike. I arrived at the scene as Robin had passed out from fear and Matthew was being taken by helicopter to a trauma center. While I managed to focus on what needed to be done for Robin and her family, I kept thinking of the irony of the conversation we had just had regarding Jena.

Matthew never regained brain activity. The following days were spent trying to comfort my children, Robin and her family as their last moments with Matthew was sadly cherished.

On Thursday, AmyBeth and I planned to attend Jena's wake and then go on to the hospital to spend time with Matthew. Robin called as we were getting ready to leave for Jena's wake. Matthew had passed away.

Between the tears, Robin told me she had been thinking about AmyBeth's friend, Jena. This was the first time we had spoken about the irony of the conversation we had just before Matthew's accident. Although, I am sure we had shared similar thoughts through glances. Robin had thought about Jena and was planning to donate Matthew's organs. She also asked me to share this with Jena's mother along with her sympathy when we got to the wake.

While nothing can take away the painful sorrow of losing these two beautiful children, through the beauty of organ donation and prayer, Jena and Matthew's lights still shine.

Once again, thank you for prayers offered in remembrance of Matthew. Please know our family continues to keep the "Bishop Dunn family" in our prayers as well.

Margie

I began to realize that nothing is coincidental.

Jena lived in truth, which was another life lesson I have learned. She would just ask people if they noticed the beauty in their own lives, and she reminded them how special that beauty is. Jena could point out the most magnificent colors in a rainbow and yet never see color in people. She saw their hearts, and they saw hers. She could and would debate that issue with anyone at any age. Jena could hold her conviction with adults who had limited insight into people and were closed-hearted to the truth of love. She knew that color was a way of describing beauty but not a definition of a person.

Once when I was out of town, she called me frantically, saying, "Mommy, tell me I'm right, just tell me I'm right!" She went on to explain that she was in a heated argument regarding love, relationships, and that the color of a person did not matter. I told Jena that she already knew what was right and that if she needed me to reassure her, maybe she was questioning her own beliefs. She cried and said she was sure of her viewpoint but that her feelings were hurt because she couldn't believe that people she loved could look at the world so differently. When I got home, we talked more about it. I told her how proud I was that she had stood her ground with four adults who, unfortunately, saw the world with different eyes. She hugged me and told me she liked that we had the same eyes.

Chapter 24

It should be snowing. It's winter, it's New York; yet the rain is coming down like a mist. The air is too warm for this time of year. Nothing looks new or crisp as it should. It is dreary. Everything looks dead. There are no leaves left on the trees; old, brown leaves take over the once-lush green that covered the ground just a few months ago. No life seems to be in evidence outside my window or inside, for that matter. My vision seems to be getting clearer as my eyes fill. My eyes can't hold back the tears, and they let one roll down my cheek. Surprisingly, I can feel the warmth as it drops onto my lap. The tears start coming faster, one after another, but I still don't move. I see more clearly through my tears. I think to myself how cruel life can be.

Chapter 25

In the weeks and months after the funeral, I was inundated with calls from friends and family who just had to tell me a story about how they found this certain penny in the strangest place, and they just knew it was from Jena. One person had found it in the center of her bed after she had just finished making it; the other had found one on the counter where she was sure it had not been a minute earlier.

Everyone seemed to know the story about the penny we found at the funeral home.

After the burial, 500 plus people had gone back for fellowship at St. Mary's Hall. I barely remember the day, only that I was holding a picture of Eric and Jena in my hand. It was the very same picture I had taped to her bed in Pittsburgh so all the doctors and nurses could see how beautiful she was and what a great smile she had and that she was so much more than what they saw all hooked up to tubes and machines. This picture was like a security blanket for me, and I knew that. I told myself I would throw it away at the end of the day. I was trying so hard to work at moving forward.

At the cemetery, it was windy and the picture almost fell into the newly dug hole, the hole where Jena's wrapper would be placed. I was so thankful when I grabbed it quickly before it fell in. I held it tighter the rest of the day until we got to the hall. People were all around us, wanting to console us, but somehow it was more like we were consoling them. They had lost her too, and they were in so much pain. I had placed the picture on top of a pile of sympathy cards next to the plate of food that someone had brought me, so I could hug and console those who needed it. My childhood friend Debbie had given me a small angel that I was also holding on to and I placed the angel on top of the picture so I wouldn't lose it. I don't know how much time had passed, but people were leaving, and I was still standing in the same place, holding people as they came to comfort me. I looked down, and the plate of food I had never touched was now gone, and the table had been cleared. The sympathy cards were there and so was the angel, but the picture of Eric and Jena was gone.

I panicked. I looked under the table, on the floor, on each chair and there was no picture to be found. Within seconds I had half a dozen people also looking for the picture.

"I was the one who was supposed to throw it out!" I cried.

"We'll find it," Tara said, not really sure she could keep that promise.

People were now looking through the garbage for the picture of Eric and Jena. I had alarmed just about everybody left in the hall. There I was, a mother who just buried her child, and all I wanted was to have this picture back. I knew it was just a picture, but *I* was the one who was to decide when I was ready to throw it out. It should have been my choice. I needed to control at least something. I was going to let the picture go, damn it; at least let me control a picture. I knew I was out of control, and I knew it wasn't pretty. Just then Tara's son Dean came over to us.

"Mom," he said. "You have to see this."

She looked over at him as if to say, "Not now."

But Dean grabbed her arm and brought her over to what seemed at first glance to be a spill of wine or soda on the floor. She looked down at the mess on the floor and looked up at me, her eyes wide. I walked a few steps closer and couldn't believe my eyes. There on the floor, under a table, was a penny, and it was in the center of a perfect heart-shaped spill of wine.

You could not have drawn a more perfect heart if you tried. Jena and I used to tell each other, "Heart to heart, that's what we are," and there on the floor was my answer. I knew Jena left that message for me that day, to remind me—because I had obviously forgotten—that she and I are "heart to heart," and no thrown-out picture could prevent us from staying that way. I no longer needed my security blanket picture; my penny from heaven told me we would forever be heart to heart.

That would be the perfect story of pennies from heaven, but Marc's story is even better.

It was late one Thursday evening in May, and my cell phone rang.

"You won't believe this one," Marc blurted out.

"Try me," I dared him.

"I just picked up the RV in Jersey, and I was thinking of Jena and missing her. I thought I felt my cell phone vibrate, so I picked it up and saw that no one had called. You know how I have that picture of her on my phone?" He paused for me to answer.

"Yes ... yes ... I know *and* ..." I coaxed him along.

"Well, I look at her picture, blow her a kiss, and tell her I miss her. I close the phone, put it back on my hip, and I keep driving along. I put on old country music just like she and I used to sing to, and I swear I felt like she was with me. I say out loud, 'Jena J in the RV' and just then I hear a loud *ping!* on the dashboard. It startles me, and I almost drive off the road. I look down, and smack in front of me is a shiny new penny—heads up! Can you believe it?"

My mouth was open as he was telling me this. I didn't even get a second to respond before he added, "No sooner I say, 'Hey there Jena J' and another one falls out of nowhere!"

"Wow!" was the only thing I got in.

"Well, I just had to tell you. I'll be home in about an hour."

I love that story, but it doesn't end there. A few weeks went by, and Marc needed to go pick up the RV from people who had rented it at West Point for a graduation. It was only about a forty-five-minute drive south, and Marc and I hadn't spent much time together lately, so I agreed to go. I hated riding in the RV. It hurt too much, knowing the only reason we got it was Jena. We were trying to sell it, but something that big doesn't sell overnight, so in the meantime we were still renting it out.

It was a beautiful spring afternoon, and we got to West Point in no time. Marc checked around the RV to make sure everything was in order before we left. I thought of his story about the pennies, and I searched the compartments above the dashboard to see if I could see anything. Nope, nothing; I just saw a matchbook and a plastic straw. I put my hand in and felt around, just in case I'd missed something. Nope. I pulled down the visor and checked there, too. Nope, no change to be found anywhere. OK, my own inspection was complete and off we went. We talked about Jena and the RV. Marc agreed it was time to sell it, and he was sad about all the memories we wouldn't be making in it anymore. Just as he was talking …

Ping!

… out fell a penny, landing directly in front of him on the dashboard—heads up. We looked at each other and smiled.

"You're right, Jena" he said, looking out into the sky, and continuing to talk to her. "We'll still make memories wherever we go. I love you, too. Jena J in the RV again!"

I grab the penny and look at the year. It's 1967, the year Marc was born. I know that penny was for him, and I know it came from Jena.

When we got home, I ran upstairs and put the penny in my special rose box, where I keep all my pennies from heaven. It's the best investment plan for the past I can think of.

Chapter 26

"Margarete, I have a question to ask you …" my friend Kathy Mackey said, almost afraid of the question, because it was December 17, only a week after the funeral. "You can say 'no.' But I have to ask."

"What, Kath?"

"The Milton girls want to take you out to lunch," she blurted quickly.

Kathy's daughter, Sara, is one of The Milton Girls and The Milton Girls had known Jena since preschool.

The Milton Girls are the girls who knew her secret purpose in life; the Milton girls made Jena laugh, and Mrs. Bliss would take The Milton Girls to see Jena every time she was in the hospital. Denise is our dear friend and Matt's mom. Matt and Eric have been friends since the second grade and Jena—or Jena-bean, as Denise called her—was like the daughter Mrs. Bliss never had.

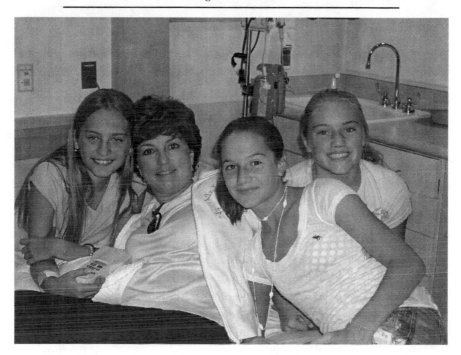

The Milton Girls were in so much pain right now, and I was scared I couldn't help them. Yet they wanted to have lunch with me.

They were pretty incredible friends who were reaching out, and I was scared to death to see them. How could I possibly say 'no'? I agreed to a lunch on December 28.

There are eleven girls and one boy—Michael. They are "The Milton Girls plus Mike." I love them all. I decided I would make a gift bag for each of them. In each bag, I placed several small gifts with a brief explanation:

Dear Milton Girls,

Some of the most important lessons I learned in life were from Jena. I learned how important your time is and who you share that time with. Thank you for sharing your time with Jena.

Here are a few things I'd like to give you:

A Penny

I included a poem about pennies from heaven that I found on the Internet.

A Mirror

So you can always be reminded that beauty comes from the inside out and that you are beautiful through and through, and remember to be true to that person staring back at you.

A Journal

So you can write your own story, knowing you are special because you are you. Your life is worth writing down so you can look back and remind yourself how wonderful you truly are.

A Peppermint Patty

So you can remember the story of Jena. The "good" stuff is the candy part. Jena loved Peppermint Patties. The "good" stuff is who you are on the inside. The "wrapper" just holds in all the good stuff. Sometimes wrappers get torn and ripped and just can't hold the good stuff anymore. Jena's wrapper was a beautiful thirteen-year-old girl, but her "good stuff" will always be with us. So remember that next time you eat a peppermint patty.

Jena's Picture

So you always remember how you touched the life of my daughter, and for that I will be forever grateful. Thank you for being her friend and loving her for who she was because that is why she loved each one of you. You will forever be special in my heart.

I would love it if you could let me know how things are going. Jena valued your friendship so very much, and it would be nice to stay in touch.

Thanks.

Margarete Cassalina

December 28 arrived and I was sick to my stomach. I had my morning glass of wine and got dressed. I didn't know how this lunch would turn out, or even if it was such a good idea. How could I help them when I couldn't even help myself? I have no intention of eating and wonder if I'd be a bad role model if I just ordered wine for lunch.

I pulled myself together and took a deep breath. I grabbed the gift bags and had Marc drive me to the restaurant.

The Milton Girls were all there with their moms by the time I arrived. They had tears in their eyes, too, as they jumped out of their chairs and hugged me tightly. Somehow we made it through lunch, and they opened their gift bags. They loved them.

We all pinky promised to meet once a year for lunch, every December 28, so we can update each other on our lives. They are great girls from great families, and they will be fine. I know a pinky promise is better than any contract, and I know why these girls plus Mike were so special to Jena.

Chapter 27

I'd been fired, let go, no use for me anymore. I'd lost my friend, my fashion consultant, and my book club president. I'd lost my drive, my meaning, and my purpose. I was lost. I was completely and utterly lost.

I found no reason to get out of bed, no reason to discriminate between drinking coffee or wine at 9 AM, and I found no reason to shower, get dressed, or eat. I had no reason to answer the phone or clean my house, and I found no reason for a schedule. Ha! Those who know me know how ridiculous that may sound. Me without a schedule is like me without my daughter Jena and that is exactly what I am.

I am me … without.

Chapter 28

Opening my eyes this morning was easy, but getting me out of bed was not. It was March 13; today was Jena's birthday. She would have been fourteen. She had such conviction that CF would be cured by the time she turned sixteen. I still hang on to her dream. To know Jena was to know that she could make anything happen. I thought I would spend this day in bed, drunk, with a box of tissues, taking turns sleeping and crying. It would mostly have been a pity party for me instead of a celebration for her. I'd even cleared my calendar in advance to plan for a day of misery.

Fortunately, the universe had different plans for me. We were invited down to meet United States Senator Lisa Murkowski from Alaska, who had arranged to have the nation's flag fly over the US Capitol building in memory of Jena's birthday. I knew Jena wouldn't let her day go by without a major event such as that. No way, not my daughter. What an honor to have such a symbolic gesture for her birthday. The flag was flying high, waving to us in the wind, complementing a beautiful warm blue sky for all to see: Happy Birthday to our own "Flying J."

Marc, Eric, and I had left New York around 10 PM and had arrived in the outskirts of Washington DC about two o'clock in the morning. The three of us, all bleary-eyed, crashed at a Holiday Inn Express off I-95. We woke up to a beautiful spring day. It was nothing like my original plan of Ernest Gallo and a box a Kleenex. I slowly got to my feet, tiptoed past Marc and Eric, and made my way to the shower. I began to sing "Happy Birthday" to my baby girl, and my tears mixed with the water. I started to smile as I thought of Jena. I finished the song and added, *"Are you one? Are you two?"* and so on, as she had taught me at her fourth birthday party. I sang, I cried, and I was happy, knowing Jena would be happy that I was still the first person to sing her "Happy Birthday" on her day.

Marc, Eric, and I met Senator Lisa Murkowski, thanks to Danielle Holland, congressional staffer to Murkowski. Danielle's parents are from Milton, and they had heard about Jena and wanted to do something special. One thing led to another and we got an invite to go to DC to see "Jena's flag" and meet the senator and Danielle, who made Jena's birthday momentous.

Chapter 29

"Daddy's home!"

"Daddy's home!" I said, jumping up and down in the doorway when Marc came home from work.

"What's that smell?" was his first response. "What's going on in here?"

Not exactly what I thought he'd be saying.

Let me back things up a bit. You see, Jena, when she could, would meet Marc at the door every day like that. Smiling, jumping up and down, saying, "Daddy's home! Daddy's home!" It always made his day. For some reason, while I was cooking dinner that night I heard a soft voice in my head and had a thought of Jena running to the door doing her normal routine. I thought, *Why not?* So in honor of Jena, I went to the door and began her routine. Marc walked in and smelled an antiseptic smell—the combination of latex, alcohol, and cotton. That smell I have claimed to be my "Jena smell." It's the smell I had smelled for weeks when no one else seemed to have been able to smell it. I swore to everyone that it was Jena's way of letting me know that she was still with us and that she was OK. No one believed me. But now *he* had smelled it. He said it smelled so strong he thought I had spilled rubbing alcohol or something similar by the doorway. When he asked if I could smell it and realized that I could not, his eyes welled up with tears. It was the first time he smelled Jena and knew she had met him at the door—again, as always. Once again, we were reassured that love knows no boundaries, and love never ends.

How *are* you?

After the funeral, it was a question I was asked nearly every single day. It was hard to explain to people how I was doing when most of the time I had no idea myself. It changed from moment to moment.

People asked how Eric was dealing with everything. After all, "He has CF too," I was also reminded daily. Yes, I knew. He knew. What we didn't know was how we were supposed to keep on living when a major definition of who we were was gone. My daughter was gone and so was his sister.

How was I?

I had no idea.

Crying was hard and laughing hurt. Yet I did them both each day. Changes I had made in my life I assumed would now remain permanent— like the tissue box in every room and in my car and at my desk at work. I wore waterproof eyeliner and mascara to avoid constantly redoing my makeup.

People told me they were sorry if I started to cry or that they were worried that if they mentioned Jena's name or told a story about their child it would make me cry. What they didn't seem to understand was that I cried when I saw the sun break through the clouds and shine a ray of light on the Earth, as though God and Jena were saying "Hello." That I cried whenever I heard songs by Tim McGraw or Alan Jackson or that I cried myself to sleep because I couldn't kiss Jena good night. That I smiled when I looked at her pictures or let out a deep sigh at the sight of a rose. The fact that I couldn't even speak when I saw her girlfriends, Meaghan, Caitlyn, and Yoo-Nah, who are officially the JMCY girls (**J**ena, **M**eaghan, **C**aitlyn, **Y**oo-Nah) from Bishop Dunn School, was the sweetest sadness I knew.

The girls still send me cards and e-mails to keep me in the loop of their lives. Tears stream down my face as I try to smile when I see their names in the inbox on my computer and I read their e-mails over and over and over again. They loved Jena, and I cried for them.

I cried when I saw a book by Meg Cabot, Jena's favorite writer, or the next edition of Sisterhood of the Traveling Pants, the unofficial JMCY handbook.

I couldn't even walk into Michaels craft store or Target without tissues in hand and a lump in my throat. I cried silently when I heard a mother and daughter arguing over clothes in the adjacent dressing room, knowing that that was something I would never be able to do again. I wished that they knew how fortunate they were.

I cried on the first day of school and on sunny days. I smiled at a rainbow up in the sky as tears rolled down my face. I giggled at the sight of a found penny least expected and when electricity turned on or off for no apparent reason. I smiled, knowing she was always around me, and I cried because I couldn't hold her.

I was convinced this is what crazy is.

Until you lose a child there is no possible way to understand the emptiness a mother feels inside. No other loss comes close. Nothing compares. Nothing consoles.

Nothing.

I woke up with a migraine and an upset stomach. It was April and spring should have arrived, but it felt like winter. There was a wintry mix of snow and rain coming down. I saw ice forming on the trees outside my bedroom window. Yet through this fierce try by Mother Nature to maintain despair, I saw life. I saw a lilac bush daring to bud. Jena had given me that bush for Mother's Day the year before. She knew lilacs were my favorite. I had forgotten all about it until just now.

I heard Eric coughing incessantly as he woke up for the day. I knew this would go on for the next hour or so. I knew there was nothing I could do to stop it. I let out a heavy sigh as I thought of what CF assaults.

As I looked out my bedroom window, I squinted because light caused me too much pain. I'd learned not to complain about the pain I can control, and I continued to look outside. I could see the dreariness of winter pelting against my window, yet I could see life. As I grabbed the extra blanket, I recalled a poem by Walt Whitman, "*When Lilacs Last in the Dooryard Bloom'd.*" I have always loved that poem and now it seems so much more profound to me. It's about life coming from death, as spring does after the winter. As I reached for my water and took my migraine medicine, I smiled. I saw the lilac bush outside my window with little buds all around its seemingly dead branches. It was proof that nature mercifully moves forward. As Whitman puts it, "*Every leaf a miracle …*" The lilac bush that had so beautifully bloomed last spring had wilted; it had faked its own death through the winter; and now on the cloudiest and coldest of spring days it was sprouting life again. It gave me joy for today. It gave me hope for tomorrow. It made me smile as I thought of my life, death, and rebirth. Painfully and thankfully, Nature moves forward *Thank you little buds. Thank you for your lesson of the day.* I closed my eyes and went back to sleep and let the medicine do its job while Mother Nature did hers. As I drifted off to sleep, I thought of Jena and the part of Whitman's poem that says, "*… for the sweetest, wisest soul of all my days …*" and I knew when I woke up I would do my best at moving forward, slowly but surely, knowing spring had indeed arrived.

Chapter 30

Again I was running late. Eric had been coughing again all morning, and he would be late for third period. Allergies this time of year, April, are so bad for him but so was staying up until midnight playing Halo on his Xbox 360. Sometimes I didn't know what to do or where to draw the line with him. He was handling Jena's death remarkably well. He grieved, went to school, and still maintained his social life. I really couldn't ask any more of him.

I grabbed my coffee and he grabbed his books and off we went to the high school. We didn't get more than a mile down the road when I was detoured. We were told by the local police that there was a fatal crash, and a helicopter was coming. They needed to close down at least a mile stretch down Route 9W between here and Marlboro, and we had to take the back roads to school.

I stopped and mentally said a quick prayer for those involved and continued my journey to get Eric to school. We went through the winding back roads. Car after car was detoured; I am sure half of the cars had no idea where they were going. The roads twisted and turned for miles. It felt like we were getting deeper into the country with every turn. Still, the trusting cars blindly follow each other in hopes of getting to their destination. For the most part people were led to where they wanted to go. Others were led farther than they expected to go, and some would now have to find their own way out. I had been down this road enough to know how it would turn out.

Eric joked that he didn't really need to make it to school, and we could spend the day together. He was still coughing. I was still driving. It had been such a long time since I had been on this road that I had forgotten that it goes right past the cemetery—Jena's cemetery. I have not been here since

December 9, the day her wrapper was placed in the ground. I had never planned to go back there. I know she's not there. She tells me this. This I know for sure.

I continued in my place in line and made my way to the school. Eric got out, smiled, and said he'd see me later. The sun was shining; it was supposed to be in the eighties today. It was another perfect day to skip school. Jena and I would have planned one, but she was not there, so I turned on the radio to distract my thoughts. I thought of her anyway and started my drive back home; like a good follower, I took my place in line. I thought of the poor families who were now devastated by the accident that had caused the detour. I thought of what they were feeling or, worse yet, the call they would receive any minute. Tears started to roll down my face as I listened to the radio station play a country song. Brad Paisley sang, *"When I get where I'm going they'll be only happy tears ... "* I think that would be the perfect song to play at my funeral. Sometimes I scare myself with my thoughts, but I still think the thought through. I think of the people who know me well and know how happy my soul will be seeing both Jena and God face-to-face. *"...they'll be only happy tears ... "*

The next thing I knew I was pulling my Jeep Rubicon into the cemetery. I had no idea why I was even there or where I was going. I didn't know where "Jena" was. I hadn't paid attention to that detail on that freezing cold day in December. I abruptly stopped my Jeep right in the middle of the narrow drive, pulled the emergency brake up, and got out. I started to wander through the tombstones. I left the door open and the Jeep was still running. I still had no idea why I was there. I looked for "Jena." Silly, I knew she was not there. This I knew for sure.

She whispered in my ear, *"Mommy, I'm not here."*

"I know, baby," I answered her, *"but this is where I last left you and for some reason here I am."*

I heard my cell phone ring in my Jeep. I was distracted in my search and my conversation with Jena. I started to get annoyed. I searched for her again.

Was it left of the Mannese family tombstones or behind the gray Virgin Mary statue by the road? I think it was farther back than that.

Now I didn't hear her voice. My phone rang again. *Now what?* I was annoyed to be interrupted again. I thought maybe it wasn't meant for me to be here. Feeling lost, I started walking back toward the Jeep. My cell phone rang for the third time. Now I began to worry that someone was trying to reach me. I wondered if maybe I knew someone in the accident. I got to the Jeep and I was relieved that the calls were from three different people and that I was not one of those families called. For that I was thankful. I mentally apologized to the callers; I hadn't meant to be upset with them for trying to talk to me. I shut the Jeep door, released the brake, and planned on returning the calls on my drive home.

As soon as I got home, I jumped in the shower and tried to start my day over. I couldn't get the cemetery out of my mind. How could I not remember where she was? How could I not know?

With my hair still wet, I got back in the Jeep and drove. This time there was no parade of cars; no one was leading the way. I was alone. I went the long way there, past Tara's house, hoping she was home so I could drag her with me. I was not so certain I wanted to be doing this, so I slowed down by her house and looked in her driveway. Damn, she was not home. I let out a heavy sigh and kept driving. I had really been hoping she would hold my hand through this or maybe even talk me out of it. I guess I needed to get where I was going alone.

I made the left into the entrance of St. Mary's Cemetery and drove along the many rows of countless stones and names. Some of the names I recognized, but most were strangers. Strangers, I thought. I thought that someone would drive past my daughter's name and not know who she was. How dare they! Then again, how dare I?

This time I found her name. I had been confused earlier because her name wasn't next to any of the newly dug rectangular mounds of dirt that are in between the perfectly manicured grass. This brown mound was where I thought Jena was. After all, it was all so new. No, Jena was not there; that one belonged to someone's loved one named "Dawn."

I found Jena's nameplate next to "Dawn." Jena *was* the manicured grass. She had been there long enough to have life growing above her. In the five months since her burial, the earth had settled and Nature moved forward. Why does Nature move so effortlessly while my broken heart was still so painful?

I saw that someone had put her name on a metal plate and there was a cross made of palm in a vase. It must have been there from Easter. There were letters in a plastic bag from The Milton Girls plus Mike, who had come out here to sing her "Happy Birthday" and had left her birthday cards. There was string still left over from her balloons. I bet they were blue and maybe purple, too. Kathy told me they had cupcakes as well. I bet they were chocolate.

Jena's girlfriends and Mike had had the need to come out here in March to wish her a happy fourteenth birthday while I fled to DC with Marc and Eric. I guess we all were where we needed to be. I started to cry again as I thought of all the people who loved her and were missing her infectious smile. They, those who were brave enough to come out here, took care of her body's resting place, and for that I was thankful. I couldn't; this I know for sure.

I sat on the grass and closed my eyes. I thought of Jena below me and above me. I heard the birds singing. The warmth of the sun felt like a hug from God, and I smiled. After a few minutes, I gathered up the things that needed to be saved and walked back to my car. I wished with all my might that I could hug Jena right then. I wished I could hear her sweet voice tell me she loved me. It hurt so much to be so close to her and yet so far—just beyond breathing.

As I pulled out to leave, a sand-colored van pulled alongside me. It was Larry. Larry runs the local funeral parlor. Jena's funeral parlor. Larry had tenderly walked us through the whole process back in December, from putting the obituary in the paper to letting us know when it was time to leave the church. He even drove to the airport at four in the morning to take Jena's body home from Pittsburgh. Larry will forever have a special place in my heart.

"Hey there," he said with a smile. My emotions were overwhelming, and I couldn't answer with words, so I answered with tears streaming down my face and a wave. I tried to smile, but my lips were trembling as I tried so hard to hold back the lump in my throat and the breakdown I was about to have. He knew my heart was broken.

"I love you," he said softly. I don't know if he remembers that or if he even knew how much that could possibly have meant because right then and there, God's grace proved how God can use people. I know Jena and God worked something out that afternoon so I could hear those exact words at that exact time. I know my heart is healing ever so slowly. I know Jena is with me always.

I couldn't even say a word to Larry. I just did my best to smile, giving him a knowing nod, and crying.

Thank you, God.

Thank you, Jena.

Thank you, Larry.

Chapter 31

It was 12:02 PM, and my phone rang.

"Hello?"

"Have you got a minute?" my friend Melissa asked. "I want to stop by and drop something off."

"Sure, I'm here all afternoon. I just need to run out and pick Eric up," I answered, my mind wandering to what she was up to.

It seems that so much of my days now have freed up and I haven't found much to do to fill them. Filling them with mundane busywork isn't my thing; I am in search of something with meaning. The days go on and on, and it seems most of my purpose is behind me. "Meaning" apparently consists of going out to lunch with friends and spending mornings struggling to get out of bed. I know I need to release some stress and give myself an outlet from the roller coaster of my emotions. *In time,* I keep telling myself, I'll know "meaning" when I see it. For now, my afternoons are free, and it would be great to see Melissa.

I like Melissa. I've known her and her husband Brian for about ten years now. Their son Brian is two years older than Eric and their youngest son Brandon is the same age as Eric, and their daughter Ashton is a year younger than Jena was.

Melissa tells it like it is. She's a-what-you-see is what-you-get kind of friend. She keeps things honest, and she is a great friend to have.

She was going to drop Ashton off to get her nails done at three that day, and then she'd be over. Her tan Mercedes station wagon was already in the driveway when I came home from getting Eric. She waited to get out of her car until I reassured her that Bullseye, our dog, could not reach her. We had

Installed an invisible fence so people were safe from slobbering "hellos" from our well-meaning dog.

"Are you sure?" she asked hesitantly, looking in Bullseye's direction.

"Yes. See?" I showed her how Bullseye was happily sitting on the lawn.

"Good," she giggled and got out of her car.

Eric said "Hello," and she asked how he was doing. He gave his teenage one-word answer of "fine" and asked how Brandon was. Brandon was away at a prep school in Connecticut and would be home soon for the summer. Eric and Brandon talked on the computer if they both happened to be on at the same time and saw each other when they could. They had been closer when they were both in the same school. Still, they had a lot in common, and they stayed in touch as much as two teenage boys do.

I invited Melissa in, and she said she had to get going but wanted to drop something off. With that, she pressed a button on her key chain and the back hatch to her car slowly lifted. We walked toward the back of her car.

"What did you do?" I asked with a smile, knowing that she had done something special.

"I got you some rose bushes," she said matter-of-factly.

"Melissa, that is so sweet of you!" I said as I walked over to hug her. She knew that roses were the symbol of cystic fibrosis.

"I got you sixty-five!" she added.

"What?"

"Well, I only have thirteen here with me now. I figured thirteen is how old Jena was and she was born on the thirteenth, so I got you thirteen to start with. I'll bring you the rest when you decide where you want them."

"What?" I said again. "Are you kidding me? Sixty-five? Really?" I started to cry.

"Cool," Eric added. His head nodded in approval.

"Sixty-five—when you're ready," she said as she started taking them out one by one. A few rose bushes were lying on their sides, and there was dirt all over her car. I told Eric to go inside the house and get a broom or something to help clean up the mess.

"Don't worry about it," she waved Eric away. "I'll do it later or Brian can," she added, and she meant it. She didn't care about dirt or a mess. She cared that she was my friend, and she knew how much her gesture meant to me. I hugged her tightly and she gave me the last rose bush from the car.

Cystic fibrosis might have taken Jena's life, but sixty-five rose bushes will honor her soul. Those sixty-five rose bushes will be a tranquil place for me to search for purpose and meaning. It will also be a great reminder of how special my friend Melissa is.

I decided to put them in the front yard next to the stone wall. That way I could see them every morning and share them with everyone who passed by. That's what Jena would want me to do. She would want me to share a smile with everyone who could see beauty.

Chapter 32

It's not what I am doing, but what I have left undone. Me. I have left me undone. I need to take better care of me. I am not a very good friend to myself, so I decided to go back to the gym today; to begin working out my friendship.

It's been four months since my last workout. Seems like a confession, doesn't it? *Forgive me Father for I am fat.* In some way I guess it is a confession. I confess I haven't gone to the gym in months; I confess I haven't cared about myself for even longer; and I confess I don't even care that it shows.

It's ridiculous and wasteful to pay monthly for a gym membership that I don't use—a gym membership that I really could and should use. But what's even worse is that I simply choose not to give a damn.

More than the number on the scale, the thing I like least about myself is mental. It is when I am given a choice, have the gift of choice, which I have control over, I still choose not to follow through. I had no choice with Jena; I had no control. I hate that. So by me not making a choice, I have made the choice, and I choose to be lazy. Lazy to me is a four-letter word—a word I really don't like.

I need to start being nicer to myself, so here I am about to walk into the gym, praying I have the courage to follow through and get in shape.

Getting into shape seems like a never-ending process. I need to get into shape both physically and mentally—a daunting feat, but still a necessity. I am now ready to put my body through hell. I want to push my body to its limits, tear down what I have inside, and build myself up to the somebody I'd like to be.

I've consciously and unconsciously ignored the signs that brought me here. My heart pills no longer keep my heartbeat regular; my ability to focus is unpredictable; I can't seem to get out of bed before ten anymore; and even my fat clothes don't fit me. I don't like where I am going, and I don't like who I am becoming, and I don't like what I see in the mirror.

I have drawn the line in the proverbial sand, and I am willing to go through bouts of pain, fatigue, and torture to get where I want to be. I know that one day I will wake up and have less useless baggage to carry around, have more mental clarity and energy, and feel strong enough to take on any marathon life can dish out.

Can you hear that? Can you hear the Rocky music playing? "... *getting stronger now* ..." It worked for Sylvester Stallone; why can't it be for me, too? It's a great movie and metaphor for life; and I am talking about the original Rocky movie, of course.

I am sure God must have liked the movie, or at least its metaphor. God must have always wanted me to get into shape, too. Why else would He have allowed me to go through so many difficulties in life: divorced parents, congenital heart issues, dyslexia, living on my own at sixteen, bad relationships one after the other, pregnant before I was married, and now dealing with the fact that I cannot hug my precious daughter ever again in my lifetime because a horrendous fatal genetic disease stole her from me.

Each obstacle I stumbled over I thought that would be all I could take, but God gave me heavier weights, and they got harder to move. He forced me to run on empty longer than I would ever have attempted on my own. He knew I would become stronger than I ever thought possible. He knew that something existed inside me that I never suspected. He believed in me; He had faith in me; He never abandoned me.

Fortitude invaded my soul, and heroic endurance emerged. Perseverance and strength consumed my spirit as I conquered demon after demon, challenge after challenge. How do you come back from losing your daughter? It goes against the sequence of the world. No one would have faulted me if I had shriveled up and died or eaten myself into a coma. But I figured if God had faith in me, then maybe I was worth caring about. I started to be a better friend to myself, and I walked back into the gym. I knew I could do it. I had God—and now I had Jena—on my side.

Be better, not bitter.

Hardships will come, but it's how you react to them that counts. The answer is entirely up to you. I used to tell the kids, "Pain is inevitable, but misery is optional." I guess I need to take my own advice, grab a gray jogging suit, eat a dozen raw eggs, and start training.

I think I hear the music starting up again.

" ... *gonna fly now* ... "

BEYOND BREATHING
By Margarete Cassalina

Beyond Breathing is a story of a mother's loss of her 13 year old daughter, Jena, to Cystic Fibrosis, a fatal genetic disease. Her journey takes you from unfathomable heartache to love and understanding of life's realities
Through her journey, she learns that life lessons come from her children and the beauty of living and the power of love. In the span of one year, she learns to go from depression and dependency to inner strength and the realization that love never ends and that there are no coincidences. That she is beyond just breathing.

65% of net proceeds go directly to The Cystic Fibrosis Foundation

Available at:
www.BarnesandNoble.com

www.amazon.com

Margarete Cassalina
130 Mahoney Road
Milton, NY 12547
845 795-2807
Cassalina@earthlink.net
Website: www.beyondbreathingmovie.com

AWARDS:

Chapter 33

This past week has been right up there with one of the hardest. Our annual CF walkathon was to take place on Sunday, and we were knee-deep in microscopic details such as how many bottles of water were needed and who was bringing the tablecloths and whether anyone knew if we had enough toilet paper for 1,000 people. The mindless part of that was bearable; the painful, emotionally self-mutilating part was writing my annual fundraising letter asking people to reach deep into their pockets and make a donation. Their donations to help fund research, research to find the cure, the cure that didn't save my Jena.

The pain I face is that the cure *will* be there for Eric and the other 30,000 battling this damn disease, but that disease smothered the flame of one of God's brightest lights—my baby girl.

Our letters are heart-wrenching, and this one was the pinnacle of pain. Pain, Jena said, is not a valid reason for stopping. So many times I have wished I could just be a fraction of my daughter.

I wrote the letter and added Jena's picture—the same picture we laminated and used for her wake. I copied the letter 634 times, folded it 634 times, and sent it off to 634 people who have reached out to us in the past to express their love and compassion for our cause. This was so very personal to me; this was my own self-inflicted hell. The letter was similar to the letters I had written after Jena's funeral. We received over 1,000 cards and letters and I sent a reply to each one of those people with the same picture of Jena. Here I was doing it again, and it felt like hell. And I am doing it to myself.

Everyone puts themselves in their own hell at times, and right now this is mine. It's like an addiction I can't stop. I feel like I owe it to someone, maybe

Eric, maybe Jena, maybe all those other people who are out collecting money for research. I created this walk; this is *my* expression of hope and optimism for the cure—at least it was for the past fifteen years. Now it is like a painful scab I can't allow to heal. I need the cure for Eric; I couldn't cure Jena.

I know, I know, that's not my responsibility.

I know, I can't control that, I know. I can only do what I can do, and I should be satisfied with that, I know. My mind *knows*. But my mind is tricky. My mind is trying to rule my heart, and it's almost winning. I am thankful that my heart is wiser, and I need to start letting my heart have a voice. I believe it will be my only way to survive this hell.

On Monday I can let it go and let some of my wounds heal. Next year, I have decided, I will take most of "me" out of the walk. I am sure there will still be a CF walk; I just won't make it so personal anymore. I haven't quite figured out the details, and somehow I think I'll change my mind, but I will get to that later. Right now I know I need to step back, do what I can handle, and I am OK with the outcome. I'll let you know how that worked for me next year.

Chapter 34

Yesterday, Marc and I went to St. Mary's church down in Newburgh. It was First Friday and we went there because Jena's old school, Bishop Dunn Memorial, goes there, grades one through eight. The whole experience filled me with love. Father Bill is a breath of fresh air who'll lift you up if you let your own wings give you flight. The Mass made me laugh and made me cry and reminded me how much I love God. It reminded me how much I love and that love in itself is good, *positive*, and favorable, even by Webster's definition.

With renewed strength, Marc and I tackled a difficult task after Mass. A task Ann, my mother-in-law, had been asking us to take care of. A task Marc had been struggling with and a task I had just taken out of my mind—the painful job of getting a tombstone for Jena. I keep shaking my head and wonder why we even need to mark a place where her wrapper lies in the ground. Why not mark the place where she lived and *lives*? Why not stick a fifty-foot statue in our front yard for all to see? Tell those people who need something concrete (no pun intended) to "visit" right here where Jena lived—her home. They can go to where she learned how to ride a bike in the spring of '98, or where Marc used to pull her in the sled when she was too small to walk up our long driveway, or where she stalled the field car Grandpa had given her when she was ten, or where she proudly rode her four-wheeler with Eric and her cousin Dane. That is where she *is*. In fact, she is where you see her.

So forgive me that I have issues when people tell me I need to spend thousands of dollars to buy a stone to mark a spot in some damn place that Jena never went to or would ever want to!

Jena knew those people in the ground weren't there either. Why should I visit "Jena" at a place that is surrounded by bodies we don't know? That "resting" place is not her home. Those who knew her know she's not *resting* either—not Jena.

Her living place, her running place, her anything-but-resting-place is: 130 Mahoney Road, Milton, New York. She is *home*. As certain as I am of this, we are still driving north on Route 9W toward Weider Memorials to pick out a stone.

Feeling uneasy, I started thinking of Jena, and I asked her to help me through this. I begged her. I hadn't been talking to her much lately, and I hadn't been "sensing" her as much as before either. I started to cry.

We pulled into the parking lot of Weider Memorials slowly, not sure where to park or what to do first. I took a deep breath, reached for the door latch, and said, "Come on, Jena. I need your help with this. We can do this," knowing full well that my prayer was selfish and all for me, in my weak state of mind and heart.

I stepped outside, and the heat from the afternoon sun was heavy. There were severe heat warnings for those with respiratory issues. I thought of this, smirked, and let the tears build, knowing Jena was free from all that and that those warnings are useless to her now. I took a few steps toward the rows and rows of gravestones. Some were in the shape of the Blessed Mother, some were plain gray and square, some were shiny black with etched pictures on them, and there is even a three-foot-high plain, round rock for those who are really "down to earth."

I laugh, thinking Jena would find that funny, knowing some people would think it was "inappropriate." Still, I know she'd find it funny. She also knows that the stone is for others, not her, and certainly not for me. I walk to the stone that's closest to the car; it looks just like what you think of when you think of cemeteries—gray, cold, boring, and blah. I quickly dismiss it and move to the second one, where I stop. I feel a strong tingling sensation that begins in my back and simultaneously travels up to my head and down to my toes, almost like a chill. It's about 100 degrees out here; I can't possibly be cold. My mind dismisses it, but my heart knows. I feel Jena with me. My eyes catch the design on the left edge of the rose-colored stone; it has no corners, just rounded edges. The design outlines the edge with a long-stemmed rose that forms into praying hands that are holding a beautiful rose. The stone itself is no more than thirty-six inches high. It has rough edges and looks almost like half a heart, a broken heart, which is my permanent reminder. The heart rests on a base that is also a bit rough around the edges, just like Jena. That's the one Jena picked. I look no further.

Marc and I go inside where it's cool. Kurt, a gentle soul, talks us through all the details of buying the stone—the wording, the delivery, and the cost. He has no idea how high that cost is to me. I can't help think of the credit card commercial that sums it all up as being "priceless." Again, I know Jena is with me. She would giggle, knowing how much my mind wanders when I am where I don't want to be. Kurt continues explaining the process. Through our conversation, we find out that he, too, lost someone he loved to CF—his three-year-old brother. Funny who God places in our lives at appropriate times, isn't it? I have long ago given up on coincidences.

We have the basic requirements etched in the stone: Jena's full name, both of her dates—I hate that she has a second date. I ask if I can add a sentence to her stone. Of course, who will deny a grieving mother? And besides, I am paying for each letter.

I wanted to have etched at the bottom: "*When you can see love, you can see me*" to remind the loving visitors that this six-foot by ten-foot place they are standing on is not the only place you can "see" her. I knew Marc agreed with me as he wiped his eyes with the back of his hand. We decided to add on the back: "*A rose in the garden of life.*" Alan had thought of that when we were trying to figure out what to write for Jena's obituary. I'd thought it was perfect then, and I thought it would be perfect here, too. We also had the back of the stone inscribed, "*St. Bernadette Pray for Us.*" That would be from Jena as a reminder to us all. It was not only her confirmation name; St. Bernadette was a special saint to Jena.

We left there with heavy hearts, knowing it was now done. The next hard part would be in the fall when the stone would be at its final resting place. I was sure it would be another time I would find myself wandering in a place I didn't want to be.

When we got home, I got a call from Mr. Sanchez, Jena's principal at Marlboro Middle School, who wanted to know how I wished to handle eighth-grade graduation. *I don't,* I thought to myself. She didn't graduate and she never will. Why should I even go? *For everyone else? For her friends? For Jena? For me?* He told me that there would be a moment of silence for her, that the yearbook was dedicated to her, and that I would receive a plaque. *For what? What possible words could they want to give me?* I stopped for a moment and realized I didn't even want to know. The principal also told me that there would be a display case in honor of her near the art room, since art was her favorite subject. Mr. Sanchez asked if I could give him a quote to put by her picture and, by the way, could I pick out a five by seven picture to give them. This was not easy for him to ask, and he knew it was not easy for me, and we both knew I would do it anyway.

I narrowed it down to three pictures and decided to let them share in the anguish of picking one out. The quote I gave was: "Pain is not a valid reason for stopping," since that was the only thing that was keeping me going at that moment.

I was beat. I felt angry, and I felt like an inconsiderate ass who is selfish. Someone stop the world. I want to get off.

Chapter 35

It was Friday night, and I wanted to go out and have my half a dozen alcoholic drinks. Drinking made my mind slow down, and it numbed my emotions to an acceptable level. We were out to celebrate Tim and Tara's twenty-fifth wedding anniversary. They were off to Hawaii the following week, so I brought leis to get the aloha theme off to a fun start.

Cindy and David, Jo-Ann and Bob, and Joanne and Harry were all there. We were laughing and enjoying the night air at a local restaurant. Conversation was light until I let out a heavy sigh and told them I'd had a bad week. They nodded their heads and listened intently, but it was Friday night and all of us were out for a little stress release. It was then that I realized it wasn't a good time to vent. Too late. I'd said too much and I couldn't unsay it now.

My friends are great, they are the best, and they were ready to jump in and pull me out of whatever funk I was in. They are such good friends; they threw their life preservers at me and started pulling me in. They wanted to help; after all, I'd asked them to. They just didn't realize—and neither did I—that that night I would not be receptive to anything. I was depressed and trapped in mourning Jena, and I didn't know how to get out; I didn't know if I wanted to either.

I asked; they answered. In hindsight, I should have waited until our Wednesday girls' night at Cindy's, when this type of conversation would have been therapy. We'd begun the Wednesday night "prayer group" when Cindy's son Matthew went to war on his first tour to Iraq in November 2003. Wednesdays are our nights to pray, vent, talk, and have a few glasses of wine. Those Wednesdays at Cindy's have saved all of us millions of dollars in therapy. I love them all for that. I owe them the world for that.

But that night I spoke too soon, and they immediately began to help. Unfortunately, the answers from everyone were generalized, for lack of a better word. Maybe it was what I was hearing, or maybe none of us really wanted to get into "it" that night.

I know all the experts you read will tell you that when you are depressed or are in mourning you need to let out your emotions. Yeah, I get that, and I do let them out. I know I should "feel" what I "feel," and I know I should not be too hard on myself; after all, it's only been *fill in the blank.* I also know that I need to express and release bottled-up emotions or it can resonate deep within me and perhaps manifest itself in other damaging expressions I wouldn't recognize. *I know!* I have read enough self-help books to give a course. I have also read every grief book given to me in the past six months.

These ladies knew me and knew me well. But the responses I got were not what I was looking for. But to be fair, I had no idea what the hell I was looking for. Maybe it was to make everyone as miserable as I was. I am thankful that they love me enough to have forgiven me.

I knew I needed to let my feelings out and right then it seemed that anger was one of my emotions. I know that there are many different so-called *healthy* ways of "freeing" up these emotions. I could scream and cry, and guess what? I did. I could exercise, and I did. I could be creative—drawing or writing—gee, what the hell am I doing now? I could talk with friends, and I do that every Wednesday, or talk to myself, and I do that *all* the time. Like I said, I got it, and I did it.

I had no problem letting out my emotions; my problem was that I was not sure *what* the real emotion was that I was feeling. I was not sure whether my emotions were genuine or whether they were manufactured by my very own mind. I wasn't sure, and this was what bothered me. My friends gave me their best advice, and that came from their past experiences or from information they had gathered along the way, but it just wasn't helping.

Once I was back home, I couldn't get the melancholy feeling out of me. I don't like feeling this way. So my first answer to myself is, *"If you don't like it, then change it."*

I went to bed and read *Conversations with God,* another book someone had given us, hoping it would help us in our grief. I read the book, hoping to be inspired.

Ask and you shall receive.

At one o'clock in the morning the "ah-ha" moment arrived. It was not what I had read, but the combination of the whole day—the message at church, the evening with friends, the book, and, most important, the conversation with Jena that I had right before I went to sleep. Yes, Jena.

When I was talking with Jena, she reminded me that she is with me always; it is *I* who am not with *her* all the time. I had been second-guessing whether I could really talk to her and whether she could "speak" to me. I had been second-guessing myself because I was not sure if I was going crazy, had always been crazy, or was just trying to use my conversations with Jena as a means to "overcome" my grief. My mind told me this, and then I didn't know anything for sure.

I know my mind controls my logic, and what I think. The mind can control it all. But my mind doesn't necessarily live in truth. When I live in truth and joy, I don't have pain. I want truth. I want joy.

My mind gets in the way; it thinks too much, it tries to make logical sense out of illogical thought, and my heart gets pushed aside in the process. I know this happened because I do not feel whole, and I certainly do not feel joy. This I do know for sure.

I have realized that I need to be still, to meditate, and to be quiet with my self—my higher self. I start reflecting back and I know that I have not been "talking" to Jena and that I have been letting my mind tell me not to. After all, Jena wasn't here, was she? I can't see her, right? I can't touch her, right? So she must not be here, right? Yet my soul still feels her, but when this happens my mind acknowledges that she is not physically here. Therefore my mind tells me to "remember" her in thought and memories. My mind tells me that she is no longer here on Earth, and that causes me to sink into feelings of extreme emotional loss and depression, which my mind has created.

My soul knows she is around me. My soul can feel her. I have always been able to feel her in a way where words are too limited for explanation.

One example of this is when Jena used to wake up in the middle of the night coughing. If you ask Marc, he'll tell you I sleep like a rock. Nothing wakes me up.

Yet I would swear that I could hear Jena coughing in her room, and I would wake up, look at Marc, and wonder why he wasn't awake dealing with the situation. I would grab my robe, run down the hallway, and open Jena's door just in time to see her wake up from a sound sleep, just beginning her coughing spell. As she coughed, she would look at me inquisitively, as if asking, "How did you know to come in here?"

I would look back at her, bewildered as well, but I was there to comfort her for the rest of the night. This happened many, many times. Eventually, Jena would just look at me, smile, and reach for my hand as she battled those coughing spells, and I thanked God I could *hear* her when no one else could.

She is more than my daughter; our souls are connected. My heart knows this, too. The peace that I feel overcomes me, and I know her spirit is in me and around me. If the experts call that "compensating for a loss," so be it. What I do know is that I miss her, and I cry about that every day. The crying is short-lived, and I accept it. I accept that crying is now a part of my life, and I am OK with it. I also know that I quickly turn to happy memories, knowing how much I loved her then and love her still. I feel joy and gratitude, and that is where I want to stay. My memories don't make me sad. I love to hear her name, I love to think of her, I love all the feelings about her, even when I miss her and cry. I thank God for that, too. My "ah-ha" moment is knowing that love is never-ending, and when I can see love, I can see Jena.

It feels quiet in my heart, and I feel peace in my soul, and I am now learning to live in love and joy. This I know for sure.

Chapter 36

"I'm up here on the ledge!" I screamed into the microphone. I was standing on the edge of a rose garden. It was also the highest point I could stand on to be seen.

"My name is Margarete Cassalina, and I am just one of the many CF Committee members who organized this walk today."

I continued with my speech to a fundraising crowd of at least 1,000. Today was Sunday, the cystic fibrosis walkathon would be all over in a matter of a few hours, and I would feel the stress and anxiety leave my body. I would reward myself with my annual corned beef Reuben with sweet potato fries as soon as the last garbage bag was thrown away for the day.

"... I am a committee member but also a mom to two wonderful kids who were born with cystic fibrosis. Eric, standing over there by the Airgas Orange County Chopper bike, who'll be sixteen next month ..." I waved to him. He was embarrassed and looked down at the ground, but then he forced a smile and waved back.

"... and Jena, my beautiful daughter, who lost her fight against CF in December, when she was only thirteen ..." I knew my eyes were welling up, but I held my ground, controlled my voice, and continued. As I looked around, I saw that others weren't faring as well. Unlike them, I had been practicing my strength all morning.

That morning was tough. The alarm went off at five thirty. I looked out the window hoping to see sun; instead I looked out to see what appeared to be the beginning of an overcast—or worse yet—a rainy day. Lying in bed, I looked up at the ceiling and asked for Jena's help again.

"Come on, baby girl, you know how important today is, and we need it to be a nice day. See what you can do, honey, all right?"

It was nice talking to her again. It was nice to know she was right next to me while I was writing this. I know she was there. I'd missed her.

It was six fifteen in the morning, and we had a house full of volunteers. John D., who had been Marc's friend since the fifth grade, was sitting at the kitchen counter sipping coffee and talking with Dane about cars. John B., who came out to Pittsburgh, and who was Eric's godfather and best man at our wedding, walked in the back door with our neighbor and Eric's friend, John V., and his younger brother Mike. John B.'s eyes were all red and he held a handful of tissues and a small bottle of eye drops.

"Allergies are bad this morning," he said as he put a few drops in each eye.

Great. I thought of Eric, and how he would have such a hard time dealing with the day. Eric has bad allergies, too, and it affects his CF terribly. I'd most likely be calling Dr. Boyer that week. But right then the CF Great Strides walk would start in about three hours, and I needed to focus.

I looked at Mike's shirt. It had Jena's memorial picture on the front and said "TEAM JENA BELLA" on the back. Mike is the Mike of "The Milton Girls plus Mike." These are the friends of Jena who have been there. They have sung at her funeral, they have visited her body at the cemetery on her birthday, they have put together a team, and they have gone out fundraising to find the cure.

They are an amazing group of friends, and Mike is among them. I smiled at him, and it was the first tears of the day. I figured it would be one of those days, so I abandoned the ordeal of putting on makeup just to have it run down my face.

Marc was already outside and was bringing out the last of the boxes for the walk. John D. got in his truck, and the rest of us got in the RV and headed down the road. We had to stop at the Bliss's house to get Matt and the rest of Eric's friends who'd volunteered to help. There were eight teenage boys who could have been sleeping in that morning, but instead they were all up and showered and ready to go; it was Sunday and it was not even six thirty. My second tears of the day.

By the time we got to the park, the volunteers were in full swing: tents were going up effortlessly, balloons were filled, signs were in the ground. No one said it, but we all knew we were in this together. It's what family feels like.

Up there on the ledge, I could see the faces of so many people I knew who had been supporting us all those years. And there were so many new people who were just now beginning to learn about what CF would mean to their families. My heart broke for those who would go down the road I'm on.

"... Together we can make a difference in the lives of those battling this disease," I say confidently to the crowd.

"... and with your help, we will make CF stand for Cure Found!"

The crowd clapped with enthusiasm. Twelve-year-old Ali Peratikos sang the national anthem so beautifully it sent chills down my spine. When she was done, the walk began. It was a good day. While the walkers and a few runners were on the three-and-a-half-mile trail, working off some emotional energy, Michelle and Mary were counting money and punching away at calculators trying to come up with a fundraising figure we could give the crowd when they returned.

Michelle works with Mike and Marc at Merrill Lynch and Mary has been Mike's girlfriend for the past eight years. Michelle and Mary are also dear friends who have done the CF Great Strides registration at the walk since we started doing it years ago. They were there because of love. Love for us and wanting to make a difference. I knew better than to even look in their direction until they were done adding. But they knew me better and let me hover over them anyway.

Mary looked up at me and smiled. Michelle looked shocked and showed me the number. I screamed so loud that the few people who had stayed back from the walk looked over at me to see if I was OK. I waved to them and said, "Oh, sorry, I'm fine," and covered my mouth to prevent any future screams. I couldn't wait to tell the crowd when they got back.

I saw the first person making his way up the hill, back from the walk; it was Matthew, Cindy's son. He was jogging, as though he'd taken all the time in the world to get there. No one was even close to being behind him. There were about three of us cheering at the finish line. We were jumping up and down, waving posters that said "Thank you!" and "Way to go!" Matthew grinned, took off the earbuds to his iPod, and looked a bit unsure of what we were doing.

"You're first!" I told him as I waved over the photographer to get our picture. The reporter from the local newspaper was there, too, and wanted to know his name.

"Matthew Schaffer," I blurted out. Then I quickly corrected myself and proudly said, "*Captain* Matthew Schaffer."

Matthew slowly shook his head back and forth, bent his head toward the ground, and quietly said, "Just Matt. I'm a civilian."

The photographer wanted to get our picture. Matthew looked at me, pulled at his damp T-shirt and said, "I'm all sweaty," and took a step back. I didn't care, and I tightly wrapped my arm around him, smiled at the camera, and pointed my finger as if to say, "No. 1."

Matthew is humble and unassuming. He is also one of the few people in this world I consider a hero. Matthew married his high school sweetheart, Amy, while he was in college. They have three beautiful little girls and one on the way. In between all that, Matthew also has been at war twice. The first time in Iraq, Matthew defended our country during a four-month tour. The second time, he put his life on the line for a year where he became a captain and received a bronze star medal. He has never explained how he earned it. Matt possesses a quiet sense of pride and duty. While he was over in Iraq, he kept most of what he was doing secret from Cindy and just let her know he was fine and that her son was safe. Though it was a lie, it was what everyone needed to hear. No matter what side of the political spectrum you stand on, you can't help be indebted to Matt. He's the definition of honor, respect, and hard work. He is what true heroes are made of.

And there he stood, the first runner of the day, not wanting to be in the spotlight, and yet the No. 2 runner was still nowhere in sight. It is actions, not words, that impress me, and Matthew is quite impressive. As with this three-and-a-half-mile race that he ran effortlessly and won—he's the kind of guy who'll say it's no big deal, it's all in a day's work. After the last picture was taken, Matt walked over to a very pregnant Amy, gave her a kiss, and took their two-year-old daughter, Abby, by the hand. They walked over to get some water. *When you can see love, you can see me,* I thought to myself as I watched them walk away. I felt Jena, and my eyes welled up. I smiled, looked up at the sky, and thanked the universe for being so blessed.

The last walker arrived and everyone was gathering around the rose garden, waiting to hear the tally for the day. I could barely contain my secret number anymore. Chris, the DJ, gave me the microphone and turned down the music.

"Can I have your attention please?" I interrupted the crowd

"I just want you to know that ninety cents out of every dollar you raised is going directly back to CF research. Science buys life, and you just bought a whole bunch of tomorrows for those with CF, and I want to thank you." I had everyone's attention and I continued.

"Last year we raised $170,000 going door to door asking for donations. We asked strangers and family, we asked businesses and friends. We did this because we know we can make a difference. I want you to know we certainly have made a difference here today. I have to add that the number we raised is also Jena's birthday. I know she had a hand in this—she always did. So thank you, each and every one of you, because today we raised ... drum roll, please ... $313,000.00! Thank you!"

I looked out at the crowd. They were all clapping, crying, and smiling. They felt good and so did I. It was a good day, the sun was out, and there was no rain in sight. I turned around to see Marc right behind me. I had barely seen him all day. I hugged him and cried one last time that day. I gave him a kiss, smiled, and asked him, "Can I get my Reuben now?"

Chapter 37

My mother sent me an e-mail today.

> April 26, 2007

> Hi Margarete,
> Could you send me a copy of your birth certificate because I need it for the German social security. In case you speak to Matthew I need his as well.

> Greetings

> Mom

She had never sent a card, never e-mailed a sympathy message, and never called. She had never told me that she was sorry about Jena. The only communication I received from her was that e-mail.

That was what I was to her. She needed my birth certificate to receive $25 from the German government for having me. Doesn't that leave you all warm and fuzzy?

In her defense, she was never very good at being there unless by "there" you meant Europe or the egocentric world she lived in. She was always very good at being *there*.

"Mommy's mom" was how Jena referred to her. Jena didn't know what else to call her. "Mommy's mom" had only met Eric and Jena twice in their lives and that was more than I had ever expected.

She missed my teens, my twenties, and my thirties; she missed my wedding to Marc; she missed Eric's miraculous birth; and she missed Jena's precious life. The sad part was that *she* was never missed.

I prayed every night that she would learn what love is. That love is all that matters. That love is the greatest of all. I prayed that if she were ever able to see love, she would see Jena and maybe she would hear her granddaughter then.

Chapter 38

Nine months after the funeral, in August 2007, I found a job. I was hired by the same local private college that I had worked at years ago—Marist College. I had loved working there but left in 1991 when Eric was born with CF and needed me at home, and I needed to be with him. I came back to the same local private college because Jena died from CF and I am no longer needed anywhere.

I believe in karma, destiny, and things happening for a reason. Back in May, when I knew I wanted more out of my days than going to the gym or going out to lunch, I put in an application only to Marist College. Thought into action is the only way to achieve anything in life. I felt like part of me was coming back to life, and I liked it. I like to work and I like to be productive. I wanted to work as hard as I did against CF but without the emotional attachment. As far as my efforts against CF are concerned, they will never stop. I will always be involved in the fight for the cure, the cure that has two years to get here.

It really was no surprise to me that I got the only job I applied for. I knew that if I didn't get this job I would continue my days of searching for meaning and wallowing in and out of states of drunkenness. I needed this change, and I was ready to move forward.

During my interview, my boss had explained what my job would entail. He was trying to warn me that I would face challenges, and that there would be good days, and there would be bad days. I politely told him that I had seen challenges, and I was sure I knew what a bad day was, and that nothing at work would ever come close.

Here we go again

On my first day at work, I had a panic attack within five minutes of walking into the office.

The first panic attack I ever had was right before I got on the plane to Pittsburgh with Jena. This time I knew what it was, and I had to call Marc to take me to the doctor because my heart was racing, I couldn't stop throwing up, and I couldn't breathe.

I couldn't believe this was happening. I was so excited about my new endeavor. I could now find purpose and meaning. I would now have a reason to get out of bed now and be somebody. I even went out and bought new clothes to fit the part. I told all my friends, and they were thrilled for me. They told me that the college was lucky to have me. I really do have remarkable friends. So with all this great new stuff, why was I having a panic attack?

I was so eager about what the future would hold and yet, at the same time, I was sick over the thought that I was moving forward without Jena or, worse yet, that somehow I would benefit from Jena not being here anymore. I couldn't handle either thought and wound up on the floor again with people hovering over me, checking my pulse, heart rate, and blood pressure and writing prescriptions for Valium. Lovely. Just lovely.

On the drive back from the doctor, Marc gently reassured me that Jena is with me whether I am home or at work. He told me that Jena would want me to move forward, and she would want me to be happy, and working has nothing to do with not loving her. She would never want me to stay home in self-pity. I was trying to figure this whole life thing out, and apparently, panic attacks are part of my trial and error.

I miss Jena. I miss everything about her and yet I know she is still in me and with me. I know it doesn't make sense, but somehow I thought I owed it to her to be miserable the rest of my life. I would have truly been OK with that.

Someone once told me that the severity of my grief is equal to the love I have for Jena. If that were the case, I would have stopped breathing when I wanted to, which was when she did. I know the person meant well with that thought, but I disagree. Grief doesn't have to equal love, but love does ease the grief and misery of such a monumental loss. Then I hear my own advice, and I know that pain is inevitable, but misery is optional. I opted out.

Walking back into the office, I had to face my new coworkers again. Everyone knew about Jena and they were sympathetic to my situation. They didn't make a big deal about it and let me get situated in my new job. This whole job thing was going to work out, after all.

That afternoon, Marc sent some cookies to me so I could share with my new friends; he also sent along one red rose. It was his way of reminding me that Jena is with me at work, just as she is at home, just as she is everywhere I am—always.

Not everyone gets me, but Marc does, and that is all that matters.

Marc is the smartest man I have ever met. He has to be; after all, he knows how to deal with me. Marc can do complex calculations in his head and come up with an answer faster than I can using a calculator. He has a way with numbers, concepts, and the ability to see consequences others tend to miss. He is tall, dark, and handsome. To me, he gets better-looking all the time. He is often corny, and I like that. He laughs at himself when he tells jokes like, "A horse walked into a bar, and the bartender said, 'Why the long face?'" He cracks himself up with that one. Still, I smile and love to see him laugh.

Marc listens to me, and he hears what I say. I know he loves me and not just because he tells me so but because of the little "I love yous" he does every day. He brings me coffee in the morning, and sometimes we stay in bed for hours just having coffee and talking. He kisses me each hello and good-bye and every good night. He's a great friend, and he is a phenomenal father. He continually gets better at whatever he does, whether it's his job, being a parent, staying in shape, or growing spiritually. He always moves forward, and for that I love him. We argue, we disagree, we don't always see eye to eye, but he always speaks his mind, he always stays, and he has never threatened our relationship. He showed me love I never knew could exist. To say that I love him is so limiting. The best way to describe it is that if I were blind and could never touch him, I would love him just the same. If love is the greatest gift from God, then God must be in love with me.

After my second week at work, a colleague noticed that the rose on my desk was still in full bloom and was thriving remarkably. She looked surprised and said how odd that was—she actually leaned in to smell it, not believing it was real. It's real, all right, I said to myself. I knew it was Jena J hanging with me at work. When it comes to her making her presence known, nothing surprises me anymore.

Months later, I was thriving remarkably, as the rose had, and I hadn't needed to take another Valium. I knew that my life has a purpose, and I knew I have meaning. I also understood that I don't need to know God's blueprint all the time. I was learning to trust life one day at a time. I was learning that if I had faith in myself I would be able to handle what came my way, even if it was only just enough strength for that particular moment. I lived in love and joy and knew that love never ends. People still ask me, "How do you keep going?"

I just smiled and said, "What keeps me going is knowing that it will all be over soon."

Chapter 39

It was Thanksgiving, the last "first" holiday before the "first" year was up. The first of anything completely sucks. I had always done Thanksgiving here with everyone: Ann; Alan; Lisa and her husband, Dominick, and their kids Ashley, Giavanna, and Dominick. My sister, her husband, John, and their three kids, Anna, Ali, and Jonathan used to come down, but when Ev and John got divorced, she stopped coming. Marc and I kept John in the divorce, and he continued to come down with the kids year after year; that's who was here the previous year at the last Thanksgiving where I held my baby girl.

Last year seemed a lifetime away. A lifetime I would trade everything to go back to. It was last year that Jena made us start decorating for Christmas the day after Thanksgiving—oxygen tank and all. If it weren't for her persistence we would not have decorated, downed hot chocolate, and listened to Alan Jackson Christmas songs. Jena's favorite was "Santa's coming in a pickup truck." She was so proud to be a "redneck girl," and she pushed us to do the traditions that make our family special. I didn't have the strength or desire to decorate for Christmas this year, or play Alan Jackson. I had been drinking hot chocolate but added a butterscotch schnapps liqueur to make it go down a little easier. I hoped next year things would be different, but that was something I wasn't planning. My new slogan: "Day to day is A-OK."

But today was Thanksgiving and I was not OK. John couldn't make it down and Evelyn had the kids and they were staying in Plattsburgh with her third husband, Dave, his three kids, and her three kids. Ev and I had stopped talking. I think it was because we had nothing in common anymore. It didn't seem like we had anything to say to each other, so we just stopped. The last time I had spoken with her was April, a month before she got married—not to Bruce, the person she left John for and brought to Pittsburgh in December. And it was not to John, though she had said in February that she would do what it took to make the marriage work.

We didn't see things the same way. Like I had told Jena, we had different eyes.

It was Thanksgiving and I would be with Eric, Marc, and his family.

It was Thanksgiving, and I knew I should be thankful. It was Thanksgiving, and I was not OK.

Chapter 40

I woke up one Sunday afternoon; it was almost the end of November, and it was snowing. I watched the snowflakes drifting down, lightly covering the ground. I looked at the tree branches, which no longer had any leaves. They looked cold as the snow slowly covered them. I couldn't get out of bed. I couldn't stop crying.

I should have gone to church today, but I didn't. I should have wrapped Giavanna and Dominick's birthday presents by now but I hadn't. I should be OK by now, but I'm not.

My dear friend Kathy Mackey called me this morning. She told me that there would be no one-year anniversary Mass for Jena on Tuesday, December 4, because Father Fred was still recovering from his gallbladder surgery and had canceled all the Masses for the week. He canceled Jena's Mass at Jena's church in Jena's honor.

Kathy wanted me to know, in case Father Fred had not called. He hadn't.

I wasn't crying because the Mass had been canceled. I was crying because I was glad. The whole year I had woken up every morning and thought about what I did last year at the same time with Jena, and now that thought is so viciously painful. This time last year we were in Westchester with a collapsed lung, we had a horrific flight to Pittsburgh, Jena went into cardiac arrest, and Jena was intubated. Last year at this time I was surrounded by love and pain and I had two days left of having my baby girl. She has been gone from my arms for 363 days, and today I can't stop crying, and I can't get my head off the pillow. I take pride in the fact that I am drinking coffee and not alcohol, and that's about the only thing I can feel good about.

Kathy reassured me that she loved me and would come over in a second if I wanted her to, but she knew that I needed to be alone. Eric was still sleeping because he had been playing Xbox until midnight, and Marc is out deer hunting with John D., our neighbor and his childhood friend.

After I hung up with Kathy, I call Marc to tell him and ask him to let his mother know. I can't call her. Somehow I think I will let her down. What I have realized going through losing a daughter is that you go to the core of who you are. The emotion is harshly real and severely honest. I needed to be alone. I needed to write. I needed to cry.

I didn't want to go to Mass on Tuesday, December 4, but I wanted to honor my daughter in a way that was appropriate. Appropriate was such an insult to my feelings right then. I didn't want to do any planning or thinking about anyone else. I wanted and needed to be selfish, and if it meant not doing what was appropriate, then so be it. It wouldn't be the first time I was inappropriate, but it might have been the first time I intentionally chose to be.

The plan for Tuesday—there always has to be a plan—was to go to church where The Milton Girls plus Mike would sing *Ave Maria*. Then we would all go to the diner because people were coming into town to honor Jena's passing. Then Marc, Eric, and I would go off and be together. We thought going shopping would be an activity we could do that was mindless, yet we would not be home and not be around anyone we knew.

As much as I usually need to organize and plan, I couldn't stand the thought of any plan. I didn't want to let anyone down, but like I said, mourning is so unkindly honest that it brings you to the core of who you are, and I guess I am a loner.

There I lay still in bed, bad breath and all, holding a cold, half-drunk cup of coffee, looking outside at the tree branches. The tree is the same as it was last year, but I am not. I reflect on Mother Nature with fierce envy.

I was crying because it was the first snowfall of the season, and Jena wasn't here to see it. I was crying because I should be more church-going and pray for her. I was crying because I wouldn't decorate for the holidays, and I was crying because I was hurting to the essence of who I am.

I think it hurt more then, than it did the previous year. The year before I had been in complete shock; now I was certain of what I had lost. I knew emptiness. I had fused grief into my being and I knew this was permanent.

I had accepted in my heart that she was not coming back, and I also knew I could handle it. It was a small comfort that I knew this moment's extreme heartache would lessen, and I would be able to move forward. I just didn't want to plan it.

Marc called me back and said he had just spoken to Father Fred, who told Marc that his words must have been misinterpreted. He said that he would most assuredly do the Mass even if they had to wheel him out to do it. For Jena, he said, nothing would stop him.

I let out a sigh and realized the plan would now be back in play. There would be a Mass for Jena on December 4, The Milton Girls plus Mike would sing, tears would flow, and love would once again overcome my grief.

I had learned to let the unimportant things go and hold on to what is important. I knew I would allow myself this time to cry, and things would get done eventually—just not now. I would wrap the gifts, I would shower, and I would smile before the end of the day, and this I knew for sure.

Chapter 41

Evelyn called. She said she was thinking about me and decided to pick up the phone and call. I told her she was a better person than I was. I told her that I think of her also and have picked up the phone, but the difference is, I hang up. I never actually dial; she did.

We chatted for about a half hour—nothing philosophical, just a "hello" and "how are you" chat. She was cooking dinner for her crew, and I was just getting in from work on my way out to a CF meeting, and she caught me just in time.

Little by little, time by time, phone call by phone call, we actually might be able to look in the same direction.

Chapter 42

Why did I need a glass of Cabernet and some chocolate before I could sit and write? I wondered which came first, the thought of writing about Jena, which made me need the wine, or the wine, which lets me express thoughts that, for the most part, I keep suppressed. Why do I even care which came first?

I was staring at my visualization board and noticing how much I had achieved. I created my visualization poster board with my girlfriends on one of our Wednesday night girl get-togethers back in February. I am not sure who came up with the idea, maybe Jo-Ann, but we all thought it would be great to start making our dreams come true and start moving forward in life. We all brought some magazines, scissors, and glue and spent the night gabbing away, drinking, and dreaming of what we wanted from life.

We knew that putting action to thoughts can create huge outcomes and we had a blast making the boards.

Tara put Hawaii on her board, and she and Tim went there for their twentieth-fifth wedding anniversary.

My visualization board was filled with words, pictures, and dreams. I saw that the words "distant travel" was on there, along with "a more romantic relationship with Marc", and "continued girlfriend get-togethers." There were quotes of inspiration, faith, and motivation, and I am proud to say I was in the path of all of them.

I also saw a beautiful picture of Eric and Jena with the words "CF" and "Cure" next to them. There were also the words "heart to heart" pasted right over the bottom. I took a sip of wine and turned my computer on. The writing began. I thought of the elusive cure, heard Eric coughing in the next room, and Jena, my dear sweet Jena, who was beyond breathing. I grabbed a tissue, wiped my eyes, and took another sip of Cabernet.

I thought of the time Tara had a tea party and inducted Jena into our "Ya-Ya Sisterhood" the week after Jena was confirmed. I thought of how Jena beamed knowing she was an "official Ya-Ya." I thought of how happy we were that day.

One of Jena's friends told me of a secret Jena told her back in second grade. The secret was that Jena said her purpose in life was to bring people to church. Not much of a social draw for a young girl trying to make new friends. Yet she did that anyway. Jena made many wonderful friends young and old. She had a way of touching people to their core. "*There was always something special about her*" I would hear from people who met her; something special, indeed. Jena never went around quoting the bible or trying to coerce people to go to Mass with her; she just was a little girl who knew who she was. She was a little girl who touched the hearts of thousands of people.

My therapy session began again.

I typed away … type … type … type … writing is my therapy and love is my cure.

I can't prove to anyone that Jena is here, just like I can't prove that God exists, but they both do and this is truth.

God and Jena are beyond breathing, and one day I hope I can reach a place in my life where I am beyond just breathing.

The End

(Which of course does not exist ...*breathe...*)

65% of the author's royalties go directly back to The Cystic Fibrosis Foundation toward research for the quality and control, and ultimately the cure to cystic fibrosis.

Afterword

Organ Donations

Today, eighteen people will die in the United States alone because the organs they need are not available. By the time you read this, the number of men, women, and children waiting for an organ transplant will be roughly 100,000.

According to the Donate Life American Web site, only 35 percent of licensed drivers and ID card holders have committed themselves to donation by registering to be donors through their state registry or motor vehicle department, making the donor shortage a leading public health crisis.

Organ and tissue transplants give people a chance at healthy, productive lives and return them to their families and friends. You can change someone's world by being a donor. It's the gift of life.

For information about organ and tissue donations, go the Donate Life American Web site at www.donatelife.net/.

Glossary

Bipap

Bipap (or BiPAP) stands for *Bilevel Positive Airway Pressure*. It is a breathing apparatus that helps people get more air into their lungs.

bronchoscopy

Bronchoscopy is a test to view the airways and diagnose lung disease. It may also be used during the treatment of some lung conditions.

cystic fibrosis

Cystic fibrosis is an inherited chronic disease that affects the lungs and digestive system of about 70,000 people worldwide. A defective gene and its protein product cause the body to produce unusually thick, sticky mucus that clogs the lungs and causes lung infections that can be life-threatening. It also obstructs the functioning of the pancreas and inhibits the absorption of food by the body. Today, many people with the disease can now expect to live into their 30s, 40s, and beyond.

dyslexia

Dyslexia is a learning disability that manifests primarily as a difficulty with written language, particularly with reading and spelling.

G-tube

A G-tube is a gastric feeding tube inserted through a small incision in the abdomen into the stomach and used for long-term enteral nutrition.

GERD

GERD, Gastro Esophageal Reflux Disease or acid reflux disease. Acid reflux occurs when the lower esophageal sphincter (the valve separating the esophagus and stomach) does not close properly, allowing acid to back up into the esophagus.

intubation

Intubation refers to the insertion of a tube into an external or internal orifice of the body. Although the term can refer to endoscopic procedures, it is most often used to denote tracheal intubation. Tracheal intubation is the placement of a flexible plastic tube into the trachea to protect the patient's airway and provide a means of mechanical ventilation.

Isolette

An Isolette is an incubator for premature infants that provides controlled temperature and humidity, as well as an oxygen supply.

kangaroo pump

A kangaroo pump is a device that delivers nutritional support. It is essential for patients unable to meet daily caloric or fluid requirements orally and can be provided either by an enteral (into the gastrointestinal tract) or parenteral (through some route other than enteral) pathway.

meconium ileus

Meconium ileus is a blockage in the intestines that usually comes out during childbirth.

Mickey button

A Mickey (Mic-Key) button is a low-profile gastrostomy feeding tube also referred to as a "button."

nebulizer

Nebulizers and inhalers provide medications in a fine mist that the patient breathes. Inhalers provide metered doses of medication and come prepackaged. They are portable and can be tucked into a pocket or handbag.

neonatal

Neonatal refers to anything affecting, or relating to, the newborn and especially the human infant during the first month after birth.

pneumothorax

Pneumothorax is defined as the presence of air or gas in the pleural cavity.

pseudomonas bacteria

Pseudomonas is the versatile blue-green bacterium that opportunistically infects people, especially those who are immunocompromised.

pulmonologist

A pulmonologist, or pulmonary disease specialist, is a physician who possesses specialized knowledge and skill in the diagnosis and treatment of pulmonary (lung) conditions and diseases

submucus cleft

A submucous cleft is a congenital anomaly in which the midportion of the soft or hard palate lacks proper mesodermal development, a nonunion of bone and muscle tissue of the soft and hard palates.

Resources

Cystic Fibrosis Foundation
www.cff.org/AboutCF/

Frank Deford. *Alex: The Life of a Child*. New York: Viking Press, 1983.
A memoir of a child whose brief life passage is full of meaning, faith, and beauty.

inted in the United States
769LV00003B/54/P